P.M. Dangerfield,

College House,

45, East Street,

Faversham,

Kent.

Faversham

January 16th

GW01607367

The Button Boat

GLENDON AND KATHRYN SWARTHOUT

The Button Boat

ILLUSTRATED BY SUZANNE VERRIER

HEINEMANN : LONDON

William Heinemann Ltd
15 Queen Street, Mayfair, London W1X 8BE
LONDON MELBOURNE TORONTO
JOHANNESBURG AUCKLAND

Also by Glendon and Kathryn Swarthout
WHICHAWAY

First published in Great Britain 1971

434 96535 9

Printed Offset Litho in Great Britain
by Cox & Wyman Ltd,
London, Fakenham and Reading

for
Janyth,
Elizabeth,
and
Casey

Contents

1· Bushwah

Down-river floats the button boat. In and out of sun it drifts, in and out of shade. It is a face seen in a dark mirror, a whisper heard in a dream.

"What a beautiful day," says Dicksie.

"Bushwah," says Auston.

"It is so."

The river is wide and deep and a lovely molasses brown, coiling through fern woods and muskrat swamps and moss meadows where cows meet and moo and lick salt and flick flies and think about important matters. Auston, who has never been anywhere, claims that the river is a great snake which, making a circle by gripping its tail in its mouth, holds the world together like an iron band on a barrel. If the snake ever lets loose, he claims, to hiss at a storm or bite a mountain—hold your hats, foks, here we go! To Dicksie, who has never been anywhere either, who has as much imagination as Auston but more common sense, the river is a big brown rope that ties them where they are. "I wish you wouldn't use that word," she says.

"Get me a snappier one'n I won't," says Auston.

Dicksie sighs. "If we could only go into town and talk with other children, nice children. Then we'd hear lots of new words, nice ones."

"If, if—bushwah, bushwah."

"I'm just trying to improve you."

Auston sticks out his chest. For a shirt he wears a feed sack with rips for arms and neck and some faded letters: GRO-CHICK. The GRO-CHICK swells up with his chest. "Improve yourself," he says, "I'm perfect."

Dicksie sighs again. She is eleven, her brother nine, and it is the fate of older sisters to despair of brat brothers. But as we shall soon see, Dicksie has many sighables.

A line tautens. While she backwaters the oars, Auston hops over her seat and hauls the taut line up hand over hand. At the end hangs a fat fresh-water clam. With a knife he pries open the shell, yanks out the fishhook over which it has closed tightly, drops the shell into a scatter of other shells, lets the line back down into the water, and hops back to his seat.

The button boat is a flat-bottomed wooden scow sixteen feet long and so square at both ends that only the river knows whether it is coming or going. It has a set of oars and, on uprights two feet high above each side, running from one end of the scow to the other, a sturdy wooden rack. To these racks fishlines are tied, perhaps thirty on each side, which trail down through the water and drag their hooks along the bottom slowly, slowly.

Suppose you are a clam, minding your own business in the mud. Something tickles you. You are curious. Life can be very lonely on the bottom of a river. So you open your shell and suck whatever-it-is inside to have a look or a taste and close your shell and–yank! Before you can say "Ouch!" or "What the Sam Hill goes on here?" or "Don't - catch - me - I'm - not - good - to - eat - and - I - don't - make - pearls - because - I'm - not - a - salt - water - clam - I'm - a - fresh - water - clam - minding - my - own - business!" you are out of the water and being pried open whether you want to be or not and dropped into a crowd of your relatives whether you want to be or not and that is almost the end of you but not quite.

But that is the purpose of a button boat–to catch

clams. This river is noted for the abundance and size of its clams and the number of button boatmen who live along its banks. Clamming on top of a river, rowing up a stretch and floating down again, can be as dull as being a clam on the bottom, but for children who must do it there is a small consolation. When a line goes taut it is usually a clam. Sometimes, however, it is not. Once in a while, once in a blue moon, it is treasure.

This morning, for example, besides two tin cans, an inner tube and a rusty breadbox, they fished up a flower vase. And already this afternoon, besides three tin cans and a hacksaw without a blade and a small radio without any parts, they have hooked a prize—a recent movie magazine in which, when the pages are dry, they can admire the pictures of famous stars like George Raft and W. C. Fields and Carole Lombard and Mae West. They have never seen a motion picture. Last but not least, their clam catch has been good. At each end of the scow there is a large collection of clams lying limply about and wondering what for pity's sake will happen to them next.

Auston sits down in the scummy bottom, leans back, scratches an itch, and does his two tricks. First he spits grandly over the side, ptooey. His upper middle baby tooth is missing, and his lower middle, and since his adult teeth have not yet filled the gap, he has mastered the art of spitting accurately and loudly through it. This trick disgusts Dicksie. Second, out the holes in the toes of his rubber boots he wiggles his ten bare, scummy toes one at a time, separately. It is a real feat, for most people's toes wiggle together. This trick his sister envies. "Y'know, Dicks," he says, "it ain't such a turrible life, bein' a clammer."

"Isn't."

To get her goat, he repeats himself. "Nope, ain't a turrible life atall. Sailin' up'n down a river, doin' as you please. Maybe that's what I'll be, is a clammer."

Dicksie steadies the oars and addresses him seriously. "It is so terrible. No other children to talk with or play with, we don't know any grownups but Poppa, we've never been in a movie theayter, we've never even been to town—why, we don't even belong to the world! Then there's school."

"Nertz t'school."

"Auston, you hush."

"Or maybe I'll be a Dillinger, tearin' around in a big car an' robbin' banks an' shootin' up towns ah-ah-ah-ah-ah-oh-oh!" He sits up suddenly, popping his eyes over her shoulder. "Wow," he whispers, "lookit what I'm lookin' at."

Dicksie swings her head. The button boat is drifting downstream toward the highway bridge over the river, and there by the bridge is a sight such as they have never seen.

"Hot spit!" Auston whispers.

2. Enter our hero, Whipper Smith, the handsomest, daredevilest peace officer hereabouts

He should be in the movies. He's a young man tall and slim and towhead. On his noggin tilts a wide-brimmed hat of fine gray felt and on his legs are boots of bright black leather. In between he sports a neat gray uniform of whipcord, blouse and breeches, a shining badge, black leather gauntlet gloves, and a black belt heavy with a pistol holster. The horse on which this cowboy of the road is seated glitters, the noble steed on which this knight of nowadays is mounted gleams and seems to paw the ground. It's a black and silver, eighty-cubic-inch, fifty-horsepower Harley-Davidson, the mightiest motorcycle in the U.S.A.!

Man and motorcycle take the children's breath away. Toward them they float, nearer and nearer. To Dicksie and Auston the bridge is a stage. From their seats in the scow they have often watched cars cross, and humans walking, and once even a youngster their own age who ran away when they called to him. But upon the stage no actor like this has ever strutted.

"He's lookin' at us," Auston says.

"Don't look, don't let out a peep," his sister whispers, keeping her back turned. "'Member what Poppa warned us—we're not s'posed to talk to strangers."

"Strangers? Everybody's strangers to us!" Auston argues. "Who wants t'chew the fat with clams all day? Or you?"

"Just the same, you hush."

But her brother fidgets. Finally he can't resist. "Hey there," he pipes up as the bridge looms, "who're you?"

The happy holler makes them jump. "Whipper Smith, that's who!"

"Whatcha doin'?"

"Waitin' for Dillinger!"

Auston grins from ear to ear. "Oh yeah?"

"Yeah!"

"Auston, you button your lip," orders Dicksie.

"What'd you do if he was t'come along?" demands her brother.

Whipper Smith sticks out his chest and looks fierce. "Fill him full of lead and sing a song on my sireen and take him to town and get a medal and be in the papers and run for President and beat Franklin D. Roosevelt and live in the White House and invite you over and put you in the bathtub and give you a good scrub!"

"Bushwah!" Auston laughs under the bridge. When they emerge on the other side, Auston has to turn round and Dicksie faces the young man on the motorcycle. He smiles at her. His teeth are pure white and have no gaps.

"Why aren't you in school this afternoon, young lady?" he asks.

Young lady? No one has ever called her "young

lady." She looks north, she looks south, she tries to row, but the words tickle her heart. It opens, and takes them inside to taste.

Whipper Smith perks up an interest in them. "What's your name, you kids?"

Dicksie hides her face. "Don't answer," she warns Auston. "Poppa'll whup us good!"

As the scow splashes away from the bridge further and further, Auston has fits. He tingles to talk to someone, to anyone, but remembering, his backside tingles even more.

"Dagnab you kids!" shouts Whipper Smith. "Why aren't you in school? What's your names?"

Out of sight around a bend pulls the button boat. Auston, who can no longer contain his loneliness, lets it out through the megaphone of his hands. "Hey," he cries, even though he can't hope to be heard, "I can wiggle my toes one at a time!"

3. Abcdefghijklmnopqrstuvw yz

Six clams and a tin can and a piece of window screen and a length of stovepipe later, Dicksie beaches the button boat. "Dingdong, time for Pretend School," she announces. Her brother groans.

Fetching the water-soaked movie magazine and the flower vase they have hooked and filling the latter with ferns, she leads the way along a path deep into a woods. The path turns into a surprise glade lovely with sunlight, noisy with birds and busy with bugs. This is their hideaway. Here they come each day, Dicksie gladly because it's her idea and duty, Auston reluctantly because it is his pain and torment. She spreads the movie magazine to dry, sets the vase of ferns on her desk, a cardboard box, and stands behind the desk while her brother sits on the ground in the front row. Thirty-two pupils are enrolled in the Pretend School—Auston and thirty-one beer bottles placed upright in even rows. The teacher primps her mousy hair, which is the color and tangle of mattress stuffing that mice have made into a hotel. She smoothes her dress, an old unhemmed lace curtain that hangs over her rubber boots almost to her ankles in front and makes a fine broom in back. Dicksie is a small girl, not much bigger than her brother, but gritty. She smiles.

"Good morning, dear children. This morning we will

have Reading Lesson. We will begin with the alphabet. Let me see, who'll recite the alphabet for us?" She scans her thirty-two pupils. "Will you, Auston?"

He reels it off: "Abcdefghijklmnopqrstuvwyz."

"Very good, Auston. But you left out the x."

He mashes a bug crawling up his arm. "Who needs x? I don't know no word with x in it."

"Any word," corrects the teacher. "Why, there's oodles of words with x. 'Xpect, 'xtra—there's two 'xamples." She is not certain of these herself, for she has never learned to write and she can recognize only the few words she has puzzled out on boxes and bread wrappers and in movie magazines, so she moves quickly on to another subject. "Now, children, we will practice reading." Stepping into the schoolroom she takes one of the empty bottles and holds it label-up before her brother, pointing with a finger. "What's this word? B-r-e-w."

"B-r-e-w. Hippopotamus."

"Don't be smart aleck."

Auston's eyes cross. "B-r-e-w. Submachine gun."

"You know better. It's brew." She points at another word on the label. "Now this one. C-o-n-t-e-n-t-s."

"No fair, too long."

"It is not. Try again."

"C-o-n." He gives up, spits ptooey.

Teacher stamps her foot. "We do not spit in class. Now try again or you shan't go out for recess."

Auston makes a horrible face. Either he can't recognize the word or he is about to die of stomach-ache.

"Why do I have to read?" he groans. "Them clams don't give a doggone if I do or not!"

"Because," says teacher. To girls, "because" is always a good reason.

To boys it never is. "Because why?"

"Because someday we might go into town and to the theayter and you won't even know what the people in the picture are saying."

"No, we won't. We won't never."

"Ever. But we might. And when they talk, you don't hear their voices. What they say is printed in words right on the screen just like on this bottle, and everyone reads them."

Auston is doubtful. "Whatta you know about movies? You've never been."

"I know because She told me."

With that word, Reading Lesson is over, the Pretend School closes. A sad cloud scuds overhead, casting a shadow. Birds cease to call and bugs to crawl. Brother and sister look at each other, then away. "Dicks?"

"What?"

"Say about Her again," says Auston softly.

"Do I have to?"

"Yup. You gotta tell me every day or we'll both forget who we are and where we come from. I'd just as leave forget about x, but not about Her. Please?"

Walking slowly back to the box which had been a desk, Dicksie sits down, props her elbows on the box and her chin in her hands and sighs. Auston's right. If she does not tell the story often, like a label on a bottle it will peel and weather away in the mind and they will be orphans of memory. They have pitifully little past. Let this link break and they'll be strangers even to themselves. Therefore she tells it, as she has so many times.

Jake, their father, is their stepfather. Their real father, whose name she has forgotten, and who was a button boatman down the river aways, just one day up and left when she was a toddler and Auston newly born. Why he up and left no one knew, but no one ever saw hide nor hair of him again. A little later, She got divorced from him for leaving Her and married Jake and brought her two kids to live with him in the shack. But when She had been married to Jake only two years, She died. That was the end of everything.

"You were two years old then, Auston, and I was four going on five. Next year I'd have gone to school, for She had her mind set I would, and you, too, someday because She wanted us to be somebody. She could read and write and She learned me the alphabet and told me all about school, what kids do there, and all about town, the stores and movies and people and what it's like. Just about everything I know, She told me. Then She caught the grippe one winter, and it got worser and worser and turned into ammonia. One night She could hardly talk, but She said for me to take care of you and raise you proper and I promised Her. The next day She had to go and die. Poppa started on the beer and I just cried."

Auston has listened intently. "Where do folks go when they die?"

"I don't know," she says, for she cannot tell a lie. "But long's you keep in mind of them, they don't really die, they're still here."

He thinks about that. "Like clams," he says.

"Clams?"

"Sure. Sleepin' under the river. You can't see 'em, but you keep hookin' 'em up an' you know they're there."

Dicksie nods. Her eyes are large and gray and solemn. She sits erectly and fixes her brother with them. "You see what happens. I can't even remember his name, our real father. That's already gone. That's why we mustn't forget Her. She was kind and beautiful and loving and clean and the nicest thing we've ever had in our life. If we ever forget about Her, we're just worthless, you and me. We're lost."

Auston bites his lip. "Dicks."

"What?"

"Say it. Her name."

"Lily."

The sweet sound of the name lingers in the glade. It is a cobweb of echo. It is the warmth of a woman's hand upon a child's head. It is a blessing.

And so that it may not break, or sink forever into silence, or be spoiled by other sounds, but wait there for them with their other treasures, the vase of ferns and cardboard desk and soggy movie magazine and bottle boys and girls, they tiptoe from the woods without another word.

4. In which we meet Jake, a villain, and Zip, his drunkard dog

They clam home.

Home is a wreck surrounded by a mess. The shack in which they live is built of everything imaginable—old doors, odd pieces of scrap lumber, laziness, corrugated tin sheets, logs, rusty parts of automobile bodies, carelessness, half of a billboard, a bit of a barn, chicken wire, rope, poverty, an upside-down bathtub, fence posts, earth, rubber tires—oh yes, and under one corner a cracked porcelain kitchen sink. The shack sags from the weight of winter snows. It leans against the threat of summer storms. The rains of spring have washed it smooth. From its sides and roof, weeds wilt. It squats in a cove beside the river in the center of three piles as high and wide and interesting as itself. The first is composed of hundreds of empty beer bottles, some of which have lately been enrolled in Pretend School, and the second of thousands of brown clamshells spread open to show white. The third is made of what appears to be a great, gray Jell-o glob of glue, but which is actually an icky, sticky mound of the slippery, slimy, moldy, maggoty insides of a million clams more or less. And over this pile, by day and night, hover a billion flies, buzzing with wonder and delight.

Dicksie and Auston pull the button boat ashore and

collect the day's catch in a gunny sack. Toting it to the clamshell pile, they sit and clean the clams, using knives to force them open. This is the chore that Dicksie detests and Auston enjoys. Into a shell he slips the tip of the blade, then cocks an ear, listening. "What's that? Hear it?"

"What's what?" asks his sister.

"Now!" Into the shell he stabs the knife like a dagger. "Eeeeeeee!" he shrieks. "Hear 'im scream! Eeeeeeee!"

Dicksie sickens. But her brother pries open the shell and crying, "Murder! Murder! Eeeeeeee! Eeeeeeee!" slits the insides loose and pitches them skillfully through the flies onto the insides pile.

Each shell must next be scraped, its back cracked and spread wide, then thrown onto the shell pile to dry. It is nasty work, and they have not finished when they hear the crash of bushes and the clump, clump, clump of rubber boots through the woods, and presently a man and a dog come into view, both staggering.

"Poppa's drunk again," Dicksie sighs.

"So's Zip," says Auston.

As they emerge from the woods, the hound-dog sees the children and attempts to run to them for a welcome home, but his legs bend and buckle, he reels sideways, rights himself, reels again, then falls flat on his nose in a brown heap of legs and flop-ears, and lets out a long, luxurious burp. His master aims a friendly kick at him in passing, misses, and clumps up to the workers to stand with hands on hips, swaying. Jake is a huge lump of a man, his face stubbled with beard, his eyes bloodshot and bleary. Over his boots hangs a set of grimy overalls without a shirt, so that his thick neck and shoulders and arms are bare and, above the overall top, in the middle of his hairy chest, is visible a tattoo of bright red. It's a picture of the small monoplane in which, only seven years ago, in 1927, Charles A. Lindbergh flew the Atlantic Ocean alone, all the unbelievable way from New York to Paris. Above the plane is an inscription: "Lucky Lindy."

Dicksie smiles. "Did you have a nice time in town, Poppa? Did you bring some groc'ries?"

"You tend t'your knittin' an' get through an' fix my supper. I'm hungry," Jake growls. He frowns at Auston. "Catch many?"

"Couple hunderd."

"Lemme see." Jake takes the shell Auston is about to pitch onto the clamshell pile, inspects it, grunts with dissatisfaction and waves it at his stepson. "I've tol' you till I'm blue in the face–scrape 'em clean! Nobody'll buy 'em less they shine!" With one paw he flings the shell and with the other knocks the boy a good one.

"Please, Poppa," begs Dicksie.

"Shut your trap!" roars Jake. He reaches to caress her with another good one when something alerts him. All three of them hear the whistle. Someone's coming down the snake-track road through the woods from the highway! Someone's whistling "Back in Nagasaki Where the Fellows Chew Tobaccy and the Women

Wicky-Wacky-Woo!" The road is never used except by the shell buyer once a year, and he never whistles! "Hide, you two!" Jake snaps. "Hide, quick!"

Up the children leap, bumping into each other, and head instinctively for the shack.

"Not in the house, you dumbbells!" Jake snarls. "Hide, hide!"

They skitter crazily about like chickens with their heads cut off until Auston dives headfirst onto the clamshell pile and, clawing at the shells like a pup digging up a bone, burrows out of sight inside, Dicksie after him. They hide in the nick of time, for someone approaches and a hearty voice says, "Hullo, Jake," a voice they seem to recognize. Inside the pile they squidge around in the clickety shells, inching into a position from which they can peek. Four eyes widen. They poke each other. Whipper Smith!

5. Holy Hupmobile, what's that smell!

He stops abruptly, thirty feet away, as though he has walked into a brick wall. His nose wrinkles, his ears twitch, his eyes water. "Holy Hupmobile, Jake," he cries, "what's that smell!"

"Smell?" Jake sniffs. "I don't smell nothin'."

Whipper seizes his nose. "That is the awfulest, rottenest, stinkiest stink ever put a nick in my nozzle!"

Jake's doubtful. "Might be them clams," he says, gesturing at the insides pile. "I dunno. Sure ain't petunias."

Whipper circles the great gray glob of glue. "Ugh. And those flies. Can't you hire them to move this mess away?"

"What for? Just have t'start me another one. Truth is, I'm proud of that there pile. That's ten years' steady clammin', and ten years' worth of buttons from the shells, buttons for shirts an' pants an' dresses an' whatnot. Why, weren't for button boatmen like me, half the country'd be goin' around naked as jaybirds," says Jake. "Yesiree, you want buttons you gotta have clams–an' you want clams you gotta have clam guts."

"This your summer's crop?" Whipper asks, pointing at the shell pile which, unbeknowst to him, now contains much more than drying shells.

"Sure is. Reckon there's a ton there. That's a av'rage summer. Buyer'll be along any time now."

"How much'll he pay, a ton?"

Jake spits splat. "Two years ago he gimme six hunderd dollars a ton, las' year five hunderd, this year—who knows? Four hunderd mebbe. Price keeps goin' down."

"I heard tell," says Whipper, "that pretty soon they might not use shells for buttons. They might use this new-fangled whatchamacallit—plastic."

"They better not. They do an' I'm outa bus'ness."

"Can you live on four hundred a year, Jake?"

"Not likely. Winters I trap mushrats 'long the river, most always a hunderd or so. But there's the trouble too. Las' year I got three dollars a skin—I heard this year they won't give no more'n two." Jake shakes his head and plants his boots firmly in order to appear sober. "It's a caution, this here Depression—don't know how poor folks like me's t'keep body an' soul together."

"Poor folks like everybody," says Whipper Smith, still holding his nose. "It's bad all over, Jake. Someday people are going to tell their kids about the big Depression in 19 and 34 and the kids won't believe a word of it. What youngsters in 19 and 69'll believe grown men in cities selling apples on street corners, and shoelaces and pencils? And breadlines and free soup kitchens and fathers blowing out their brains 'cause they couldn't get work or jumping out of windows 'cause they'd gone broke? Worst depression the U.S.A.'s ever had, hard times everywhere, even in our town. Yep, just about everybody's in the same boat—same button boat, y'might say."

The two men reflect on that, the one tall and young and handsome, the other middle-aged and fat and tattooed. Fidgety with waiting, Auston scratches an itch. Shells click.

"What's that?" In the twilight, Whipper stares suspiciously.

"That's rats," Jake assures him. "Livin' under them shells. I try t'keep a tidy place here, but rats ain't got no respect."

Gradually getting used to the odor, Whipper releases his nose. "Why I came out here, Jake–thought I'd never locate where you live–was this afternoon I spotted two kids clamming down the river by the bridge. Two of the dirtiest kids I ever in my born days set eyes on, boy and a girl. The boy spoke up to me. Anyways, they ought to have been in school. I figured they might be yours."

"Mine?" Jake rolls his beery eyes toward heaven. "Oh, how I wisht they was! Oh, what I wouldn' give t'have me a couple kiddies t'keep me comp'ny! Wouldn' I love the little darlin's an' fill 'em with candy an' dress 'em nice an' take 'em t'town every day myself an' see they got the schoolin' they should. But I don't, I don't, an' that's the tradegy of it!"

Overcome with emotion, Jake sinks onto the shell pile, hoping that his weight will crush you-know-who into quiet. He covers his face with his hands, his belly quivers with self-pity. "Whipper, you're lookin' at the solitariest cuss on the river. When my Lil, my dear wife, turned up her toes a few years back, it plain took the tucker outa me. I been jus' like one of these here shells—my back busted an' my guts scraped out—a empty shell, a dried-out empty shell!" Through his fingers he steals a glance at Whipper Smith, who can't help glancing at the pile of empty bottles nearby. "I know what you're thinkin'," Jake admits, "but I purely have t'go t'town now'n then t'drown my sorrows, so what? You was t'live out here in the woods with nought but a ol' hound-dog for a fam'ly, you'd guzzle some yourself!"

His young listener takes off his hat. "You sure those two kids aren't kin to you?"

"Sure? Am I sure I'm sittin' on a ton of clamshells? But how I wisht they was mine!" Jake swears. "See this here tattoo, Whipper? There was Lucky Lindy, up there on his ownsome, flyin' an' flyin' over the Big Pond an' nary a friend t'help 'im—an' here I be, clammin' up'n down the river day in, day out, no one t'share my mis'rable life." His voice rises. "I tell you, lad, it's bad enough t'be poor, but it's a darn sight worser t'be lonesome poor! Why, I was t'starve an' die, who'd dig me a grave but a dog? Who'd lay me away but the rats?"

Wakened by the wail, Zip lifts his head and howls a long, mournful howl.

His tale of woe ended, Jake snuffles, flicks away a tear with one finger and with another laid aside a nostril blows a long, suffering honk. Under him, half smothered, even his children are impressed. Dicksie resolves to forgive her stepfather and blames herself for having thought him mean and shiftless. Auston admires the performance, and resolves that when he grows up and decides to tell lies, they'll be whoppers as grand as Jake's, and as well told.

Evening glides from the woods. The cove darkens. Whipper Smith puts on his hat. He opens his mouth, closes it. He is torn between sympathy for the button boatman and a sneaking hunch that he has been gefoozled. "Jake," he says, "I'm sorry. Those two kids I saw should be in school all right, and they must belong to some clammer all right, but I guess they're not yours. I had to ask, though, and I have to hunt for them 'cause it's part of my new job."

"New Job?"

"Sure, I'm the new Peace Officer, for the whole town."

"Peace Officer?" says Jake. "What become of the Town Constable?"

"Constable shucks. Constables are out of style now, Jake. You want to be up to date, you hire yourself a Peace Officer and buy him the biggest motorcycle on the market—mine's parked up by the highway—and dress him up dandy. Put the peepers on my new glad rags!" Whipper turns around twice to show off his uniform. "Aren't I the cat's pajamas, though? Aren't I the bees knees?"

Jake stands, the better to flatter. "You sure be, Whipper. But what do a Peace Officer do?"

"Everything. I got to be truant officer for the school, for one thing—that's why I'm on the trail of those two kids. But the most important thing is gangsters."

"Gangsters?"

"You're not just a-woofin'! You mean you haven't heard of the crime wave?"

"Don't have no radio, don't take no paper."

Whipper is amazed. He thought everybody knew about the crime wave, he says. Why, every town from Ohio to Oklahoma is scared to death of gangsters and bank robbers and such-like, of real desperados such as John Dillinger and Baby-Face Nelson and Pretty Boy Floyd and Ma Barker—why, they'd as soon shoot you down as say howdy-do! They've been running wild the last year, robbing banks and breaking jails and killing policemen and citizens and frightening towns, so just about every burg in the Middle West is hiring itself a Peace Officer for protection. "Yep, any tough customers come through our town, that's my job—get 'em."

"How?" Jake inquires.

Whipper looks blank. "Don't rightly know."

"An' how come they t'pick you?"

Peace Officer Smith slaps his pistol holster. "Easy as falling off a log, Jake. Town Council looks around and says, who'd have the gumption to face up to gangsters? Who'd shoot holes in the stars if he had to, and clap handcuffs on the man in the moon? Who's the only one in the country ever put a cow in a steeple?"

"Cow? In a steeple?"

"My goshamighty, Jake, didn't you hear about that either?" An impatient Whipper pulls at his gauntlet gloves. That, he says, was the best gol-dang shenanigan ever pulled in these parts. One Halloween, when he was just a sprout about ten years back, and while the other youngsters were having their usual fun soaping windows and ringing doorbells, he had a better idea. Halloween that year fell on a Saturday night, and assembling a gang of boys, he led them to old Nesbitt Himebaugh's back lot, where they borrowed Nesbitt's young heifer. Hauling her by the tether down to the Methodist Church, which was never locked, they got her inside and started her up the staircase to the steeple. The stairs were narrow, and had four turns, and it took them most of the night, hauling on her front end and hoisting on her rear, because she weighed more than four hundred pounds, but by morning they had her tied in the steeple by the bell and Lordy-come-to-meetin', what a Sunday that was! When the bell rang or the organ played or the congregation sang a hymn, that heifer cut loose like a steam calliope! Oh, didn't she beller, oh, didn't she bawl! She ripped and she tore, she stomped on the floor, and when she was through, she did it some more! What a ruckus! And while at first the minister and the Methodists and the town were mad as wet hens, later on, when they cooled off, they had to admit it was the smartest, spunkiest Halloween stunt any boy in town had ever thunk up. So when, ten years later, it came time to pick the smartest, spunkiest Peace Officer they could, they recollected that cow in the steeple and bingo, nobody-else-but!

Whipper Smith waits as though for applause. Jake shifts uneasily from one boot to the other, anxious for his visitor to leave before the rats under the clamshell pile make any more unratty sounds. He has sobered up now, he has a splitting headache, and he wants only to have his supper and go to bed.

Dicksie, who hasn't missed a word, has indeed had to swallow several giggles. She thinks the story the funniest she's ever heard, and the young man in uniform, with his towhead and baby-blue eyes, the handsomest she's ever seen.

Auston also approves, except that if he were going to stick a cow in a steeple he wouldn't stop at one, he'd stick a dozen and tie their tails together.

Zip rolls onto his back, paws in the air, and snores.

"Nice of you to come by, Whipper," says Jake, hinting. "You come by any time."

"Thanks. Well, gotta go while I can still follow the road," says the Peace Officer, taking the hint. He starts off, only to trip over Zip. Zip yips. "Jake, you really oughtn't to give that dog beer. It's a shame to make a drunkard out of a dog."

"He likes it!" Jake protests. "Why, that hound's got hollow legs—he can drink me under the table any day. An' he's my show dog. Take him t'town an' show somebody how he'll slup up a beer an' they gen'rally buys me one too. So I drink free, an' poor as I am, I can't afford to treat myself. So long, Whipper. Don't take no wooden nickels."

"You spot those two kids you let me know, huh, Jake?" Whipper passes the insides pile, gives it a last "Whew!" and starting up the snake-track road toward the highway, disappears in woods.

Jake stands, hands folded peacefully on his belly, till he's certain the Peace Officer is out of hearing.

Then he explodes. "Outa that pile! Outa there!" he roars. He boots Zip, who wakes out of sound sleep with an arf, and as Dicksie crawls from the shells her stepfather lunges at her, swinging one arm like a baseball bat. "In that house an' get my supper, you little no-good!" He misses her, and would swing again except that another target presents itself. "I tol' you not t'talk t'nobody! I'll knock out the rest of your teeth!" he greets Auston, who bursts from the pile clawing shells every which way trying to escape the arm, only to be cuffed apple-over-cart.

For once his sister doesn't notice. She gazes into the woods where Whipper Smith has gone, on her face an expression of bliss. Dicksie has fallen in love.

6. To make delicious slumgullion, add a flea or three

There is no recipe for slumgullion. Throw whatever is handy into a pot and add cold water and stir and season with whatever is handy and you have it.

Entering the shack, Dicksie lights the kerosene lamp and a fire in the wood stove. Since Jake has neglected, as he often does, to bring groceries from town, she raises the trap door and grubs about in the cold pit. This is a hole three feet square and three deep in the earthen floor of the shack which serves as the family refrigerator. In winter, Jake cuts blocks of ice from the frozen-over river and stacks them in the pit to keep food fresh and beer cold, but by autumn the ice has long since melted and the bottom of the pit is muddy. Among the beer bottles, she locates a hunk of stew meat, half of a catfish Auston caught only two days ago, a few frazzled carrots and onions and most of a can of beans, on top of which there is very little mold. Washing the meat, fish, and vegetables in a bucket, she drops them into a pot of river water, puts it on the stove, and since she's out of salt, seasons with pepper and a gloop of ketchup. She looks about her. She sighs.

Dicksie can recall how spotless the shack was kept when She kept it. But now, despite her own sweeping and dusting and tidying up, the room is a pigpen. The glass in the window has been shattered by the bottle Jake threw at her one night in a drunken rage. Her cupboard is the space beneath the wooden table. There are as many piles inside the shack as out—muskrat traps in one corner, junk and garbage in another, and the two beds, straw ticks on squeaky springs, are heaped with filthy muskrat skins for bedding. The stovepipe slants and leaks smoke. The picture on the wall, one of the prizes they have hooked while clamming, hangs at an angle. It is not a picture, actually, but a motto, framed under glass and worked out in colored thread on cloth, and it reads GOD BLESS OUR HAPPY HOME.

She hurries next to set the table—tin plates and spoons, the last of the bread, two slices still in the wrapper, and a bottle of beer from the cold pit—and just as she is serving her men come in, Jake and Auston and Zip. Jake takes the chair, brother and sister sit on wooden boxes, Zip jumps to the center of the table and sprawls out among the plates, and some flies from the insides pile buzz in through the broken window to help themselves.

Stepfather and son do not eat, they gobble. After Jake grabs a slice of bread, Auston snatches the other, wads the wrapper and sails it at the stove. The catfish bones they drop on the floor. They feed the dog tidbits from their plates, and now and then Jake shares his beer with the animal. Zip raises his head, opens his jaws, and Jake tilts and pours from the bottle so that the hound may drink in long, thirsty slurps, after which he burps. Halfway through the meal, Zip sits up and with a paw scratches an ear frantically. This gives Auston an excuse to plague his sister. Biting down hard on his teeth, he makes a gritty sound. "Yum," he says. "Got one."

"One what?" she asks.

"Flea."

Dicksie shudders.

"Dee-licious," says Auston. "Gimme another, Zip, you got plenty. I like meat, an' there's nothin' better'n a big fat flea." Slipping his spoon under the hound's ear, he takes it out, squints, and pops it into his mouth, making another bitey sound. "Yum, yum," he says, rubbing his tummy. "That dog's really got the good ones, fulla beer, not blood. Nothin' like a flea t'put the slum in the gullion."

Dicksie's going green.

"Shut up," growls Jake, picking his teeth with his fingers. "Ain'tcha got no manners?"

Directly he has mopped his plate with the bread-crust, Jake hauls off his rubber boots and drops heavily onto his bed, covering himself with muskrat skins. Zip, who sleeps with him, tries to jump from table to bed, but since he has had more beer, his paws slip and he crashes to the floor with an oof. His master pulls him up and under the skins by the tail. As soon as Auston has his boots off, Dicksie blows out the kerosene lamp and, taking plates and spoons, steps outside and down to the river. Bending over the side of the button boat, she washes the dishes, then removing her boots she lowers her sore, bare feet inch by tingly inch into the cool water and sits with her chin in her hands.

This, each evening, is Dicksie's thinking time. Tonight her subject is "What to Do about Auston." She is extremely worried about her brother. Every day he becomes more and more like Jake because he has no one else after whom to model himself. His table manners are barnyard, his language is naughty, his attitude sassy, and his appearance raggedy. He never washes, never combs his hair. What was it Whipper Smith said while they were hiding in the

clamshell pile? That he'd spotted two of the dirtiest kids he'd ever set eyes on? Of course that included her. And when, this afternoon, Auston remarked it wouldn't be such a terrible life to be a clammer, she could have cried. Is that to be his goal? And if he's this hopeless at nine, what will he be at ten? Will he care a smithereen if he can read or write? Will he laugh at Pretend School? Will he begin to sneak beer from Jake's bottles? Will the name of Lily no longer have the power to gentle and inspire him?

She wonders. When Whipper passed the insides pile he went "Whew!" She wonders. If the insides of clams smell, do clammers also? Does Auston? Could she, even though she washes her hands and face in the river every day? And will buttons sometime truly be made of plastic instead of shell, as Whipper has heard? She must stop thinking of you-know-who and concentrate on "What to Do about Auston." She must be a woman, not a girl, which is difficult when you are eleven. She wonders. Does she dare ask Poppa again? The last time was when he threw the bottle at her. The river is so soft, so tender. Will she ever escape from it? She is so helpless, so lonely. Is she strong enough to ask again? The moon is so beautiful. Who'd clap handcuffs on the man in the moon if he had to? Who called her "young lady"? Tickled again, her heart opens wide. And then, like a blow, worry over her little brother knocks her a good one, and she is ashamed of her selfishness. She must ask again, she will ask, and if Poppa is still awake, right now!

Carrying her boots and the plates and spoons she

darts back to the shack. Inside, she gets into bed beside Auston, covers herself with skins, and senses at once that both Jake and Auston must be awake because Zip's having a dogmare. People have nightmares, but dogs have dogmares, and drunkard dogs have the worst. Zip twists and turns beside Jake, he shivers and shakes, he barks and yelps and whimpers. Perhaps he's chasing a bunny which suddenly becomes a Super-Rabbit with sharp, dripping fangs and ears like arms that reach out suddenly and seize him, grip him! How horrible, Zip yelps! Help, help, he yelps, I'm being crunched, munched, and et by a monster rabbit!

"Poppa?"

"What?"

At the sound of voices, Zip relaxes.

"Poppa, please don't be mad. But I want to ask you something. Please don't be mad."

"For cryin' out loud," says Auston, "ask 'im."

"Well, Poppa, can Auston please be let go to school?"

Her brother groans.

"He can't read or write, Poppa, and if he doesn't learn soon he'll grow up to be, to be—"

"Jus' like me." Jake finishes the sentence. "That what you're sayin'?"

"No, honest, Poppa," Dicksie begs, frightened. "I mean, it's too late for me already, and I don't care about myself anyway, but it's for Momma. If She was here, She'd want Auston to—"

"Ahem." Jake clears his throat and spits splat through the dark. The children duck. "Ahem. No, girl, I ain't mad. I guess it's the time t'tell you kids. I should of b'fore but I been so busy I couldn' get around to it."

Auston's curious. "Tell us what?"

"'Bout school." Jake thrashes around in his skins until he's comfortable. "Mebbe you got a notion I'm mean an' hard, keepin' you hid out, makin' you clam for your vittles, an' seein' you don't talk t'no strangers. But the fac' is, I done it for you–so's you don't have t'go t'school."

Dicksie is astonished. "Don't have to?"

"That's right. What folks don't tell their kids is that goin' t'school's a fate worse'n death. Or drownin'. You want me t'tell you what it's like?"

"Darn tootin'," says Auston.

"Well, know what a boogyman is?" Jake lowers his voice, speaks in deep, scary tones. "Well, what kids ain't told is, teachers is boogyladies. You get t'school an' one of them boogyladies grabs you an' straps you in a seat. You can't even get loose t'go eat lunch. Then she starts–she jabbers an' jaws an' stuffs your brain with fac's an' figgers, which you got t'remember. Now some brains'll hold more'n others, but if you ain't born with a big one, which I doubt you kids was, then you sit strapped down with your brain swellin' up an' swellin' up day by day an' your whole head achin' an' you recollect that b'loon I brung home once for Auston? How he blowed an' blowed into it till it blowed up? Well, your brain's in your skull, which is like a b'loon of bone, an' them boogyladies blows into it an' blows an' one day it's so swole up it won't swell no more an' boom! Like a b'loon!" Now their stepfather fairly shouts. "Boom! They have t'scrape your ears off'n the ceilin' an' your eyeballs off'n the walls! Boom!"

"Ah-wah! Ah-wah!" Auston breaks into tears and curls himself into a ball under the skins.

Dicksie lies still, stiff as a board.

Wakened, Zip howls.

Jake allows the children to think it over for a minute, then says, "Now you know. I kep' it from you till now, jus' the way I kep' you from school–for your own sake. Besides, I need you'n Auston t'home, an' you partic'ly, t'help me an' take your dear Momma's place." Jake sniffs. "You're all I got in these hard times, girl, t'remin' me of her, an' I love you. So let's don't say no more 'bout leavin' me an' goin' off t'school, shall we? An' you come over here now, darlin', an' give your ol' Poppa a kiss, huh, like your Momma use to?"

Dicksie's eyes are moist. Again she is ashamed of her selfishness and of her distrust of her stepfather. Getting gladly out of bed, she finds her way to him between the chair and boxes.

Crack!

He strikes her such a savage blow across the face that she is tumbled backward to the earthen floor, taking a box and the chair down with her. She sees stars. Dizzy, shaken, she crawls back to her bed.

"Now shut up an' go t'sleep, you brat," says Jake, yawning. "Any more yap out of you 'bout school an' I'll knock you up to a peak an' knock the peak off."

He yawns again and soon is snoring. In his ball, Auston trembles for a time, then sleeps.

Dicksie licks blood from her lips. She will not weep. Lying awake and somehow alone, awfully alone, in the darkness of the crowded, dirty shack, she decides. Come morning, should there be an opportunity, she will run away. She will take Auston with her, into town, for the first time in their lives. If she meets a certain someone there, and he smiles at her, that will be nice, but that is not her purpose. Tomorrow morning, no matter what punishment she must suffer, no matter what else may befall her, she will enroll her dear brother in real school.

Little does she reck! If Dicksie had even a glimmer of the dire, dreadful dangers that lie in wait for her, she would never, never go!

7. Hiss! Hiss! Who have we here? Our villainess, Diane Estelle Devere!

Through the woods, along the snake-track road they clomp, clomp, clomp in rubber boots, a button girl and a button boy. She clasps his hand tightly. He lags and scuffs and she must pull him after her. "Isn't this exciting!" she exclaims.

"Bushwah."

"It is so."

Her brother has many misgivings. Jake's out clamming, and won't return to the shack till noon, so that they have plenty of time, but Auston frets and fingers the bruise on his cheek and lets his imagination run riot. "He'll lick the tar out of us. He'll tie us on a trotline an' use us for catfish bait."

"P'raps he will me," says his sister, "but not you. 'Cause I made you do it. But when you're really enrolled in a real school, he'll have to let you go every day or that truant officer'll come after you."

They reach the highway. A car whooshes by toward town, only two miles away. Once they leave these woods and start down this highway, the die is cast, it may be too late to turn back. Auston stops. Suddenly he wrenches his hand free and claps both hands to his head, wobbling it back and forth. "Oh, my brain!" he cries. "My brain hurts!"

"Your brain?"

"It's swole! It's blowin' up already, like a b'loon!"

"Fiddle-dee-dee," says Dicksie, getting a good grip on his arm and leading him. "Come along now. Just think, soon we'll see an honest-to-goodness town. And maybe a movie theayter."

"An' a bunch of boogyladies—I can hardly wait," says Auston. "Dicks, what goes on in a town?"

"Why, lots of exciting things."

"F'rinstance."

"Well," she says.

"Hmmmmpf," he sulks. "You don't know no more'n I do."

"Any more." She sighs. "Why don't we just rest our face and hands and see."

Automobubbles pass occasionally, coming and going, Nashes and a Hudson Terraplane and Model A Fords and a Chevrolet Sports Runabout with a rumble seat and a Chrysler Airflow and a La Salle and two Tin Lizzies. Now they see houses in the distance, and a water tower, and a smokestack, and a church steeple—the one in which the famous Halloween heifer was tied?

Brother and sister fall silent. Another half mile in the warm autumn sunshine and they near the nearest house. Dicksie stops this time and, facing Auston, spruces him up. She straightens his GRO-CHICK and tucks the sacking into his trousers. She fluffs her mousy hair and hitches up the hem of her lace-curtain dress. She looks him straight in the eye. "All right now, Auston," she begins, as though she is addressing a roomful of bottle boys and girls, "we are now going into the world, you and me, into civ'lization. There's nothing to be afraid of. We'll be safe and sound and people will be nice to us if you're a gentleman and I'm a lady. You are not to spit or wiggle your toes or sass anybody. So be brave and hold up our heads and, and—" her lips quiver, "and golly, let's start."

Auston has a frog in his throat. It jumps until he swallows hard, then puts his hand in hers. Together they walk on.

The nearest house is a palace. High, wide, and handsome, with many windows, none of them broken, and made not of this and that and these and those but of brick, it stands splendidly in the center of green lawns and beds of flowers. Two tall oak trees shade it and, between their trunks, quite close to the highway, hangs a boat of netting, which is a hammock. And floating on air in the hammock, her head upon a silken pillow, is an actual girl.

She appears to be Dicksie's age, but she is as different from Dicksie as a pearl is from a clam. She has long golden curls and wears a lovely pink dress trimmed with white ribbons. Now and then she puts one shoe delicately to the ground, pushes, and the hammock swings to and fro, delicately. Now and then she sips delicately from a glass sparkly with ice. She doesn't see the two children gawking at her, or if she does, pretends she doesn't. If they could read, and if they had ever read a fairy tale, she would be the princess in it. Deep in her own delicate thoughts, she is startled when spoken to.

"Good morning. My name's Dicksie. And this is my brother Auston."

"Whatcha drinkin'?" Auston inquires. "Beer?"

Sitting up in the hammock, the princess puts down her glass. All at once she becomes pale. "I shall be ill!" she gasps. "I shall faint!" Swishing a wisp of handkerchief from her pocket, she shields a delicate nose.

"Got a gutache?" Auston asks politely.

"Ill?" asks Dicksie. "Why?"

The fair creature rises from the hammock. "You smell!" she cries, shrinking in horror from the ragamuffins. "You smell!"

8. Absolootle, positivle the worst picklement a peace officer can possibly be put into

At the west end of Main Street he sits his motorcycle, waiting. In the silence he hears his exhaust pipe, puttering. His watch, ticking. The big bass drum of his heart, booming. He sits, waiting.

Only seven minutes ago, Whipper Smith was put into what, in his opinion, is absolootle, positivle the worst picklement a peace officer can possibly be put into.

Only two blocks away, only seven minutes ago, he was sitting in the town jail, which had never held a prisoner because the town is so peaceful and its citizens so law-abiding, simply sitting and twiddling his thumbs when the telephone rang. He answered it, and went instantly gray around the gills.

It was a flash call from the Police Department in the big city. Three men had just robbed a bank there and escaped with six thousand dollars! They were witnessed heading east out of the city at high speed in a green Cadillac V-16 sedan! If they stayed on the highway, they'd pass through Whipper's town on his Main Street in about ten minutes!

"Ten minutes!" Whipper gulped. "Suffering succotash, what'll I do?"

"Saddle your horse and stop 'em!" replied the Police Department.

"I don't have a horse!"

"Your cycle, you ignoramus!"

"Stop 'em?" Whipper cried. "How?"

"Don't ask us, you're the Peace Officer over there and that's your job."

"But I've only had it a week!"

"You're lucky, you can learn the ropes fast. But watch your p's and q's with these thugs, they're armed and dangerous. They may not be Dillingers, but they'll do till he shows up!"

"What? When? How? Why? Where?" stammered Whipper. "Who? Me?" But the Police Department had hung up on him.

Whipper Smith dropped the phone–picked it up–ran around the desk one way–ran around the desk the other way–sat down–sprang up–looked for his hat–found it on his head–ran out the door–returned and closed the door–pulled out his pistol–checked his cartridge clip–put the clip in his pocket–put the pistol in the holster–realized the bullets were now in his pocket and not in the pistol–put the clip in the pistol–ran to his Harley-Davidson–leaped aboard–kicked the starter–rode off in two directions–turned on his siren–turned it off–jammed on the brakes–cut the motor and almost collapsed. Peace Officer Whipper Smith plain plumb didn't know what in thunderation to do.

Three of them!

One of him!

A Cadillac V-16!

He'd never even seen a Cadillac V-16 except in movies!

Sixteen cylinders! That sedan would do over a hundred miles an hour and his Harley-Davidson would have to hump to hit ninety!

Armed! With what–pistols, rifles, sawed-off shotguns, hand grenades, cannons? He had only one popgun!

Dangerous!

He mopped his brow. Dangerous–that meant there'd sure as shooting be shooting if he tried to stop 'em, and he must try, and if there was, innocent people might be hit and hurt, so that was one thing he could do right now–get people out of harm's way!

Kicking the starter again he rode down Main Street waving his hat and shouting. "Bank robbers! Coming this way! Everybody off the street! Get into the stores–everybody–hurry!"

He waved and hollered down the middle of Main Street, then swung about and waved and hollered up the middle of Main Street. People obeyed. Something harsh in his shout, something white and strained in his face warned them that this was no boyish stunt. Young and old, fat and lean, slow and spry, men and women scurried into the drugstore, the bank, the creamery, the dry-goods store, the weekly newspaper office, the two gas stations, the two grocery stores, the hardware, the bakery, the shoe store, and the post office. Babies and small children were snatched out of cars and rushed away bawling. Cars pulled off the street, parked, and drivers hot-footed it to safety.

Peace Officer Smith then half-circled and swung in to the curb in front of a gas station at the west end of Main Street. Throttling the Harley-Davidson down to an idle, steadying himself with one boot on the pavement, he pulled from his uniform blouse a big silver turnip of a watch and checked the time. By his best guess, he answered the telephone call from the city Police Department seven minutes ago. In three minutes, then, the sedan should come into view behind him, headed east. From this point he can see the entire length of Main Street, making certain no one enters it on foot or in a vehicle. He peers down it now. It is a deserted street. Nothing moves. Sunlight flashes from store windows behind which the townspeople crowd, behind which two hundred pairs of eyes are fixed upon him.

What will he ever, ever do? What if he just bluffs it out—mightn't that be the dumbest but the smartest trick? What if he just sits tight and when the sedan passes, rides out and pulls even with it and draws his pistol and points it into the sedan and hollers "Halt!"? Mightn't the three men be so flabbergasted they will halt and raise their hands? But then, being real gangsters and knowing he's only the clodhopper cop in a hick town, mightn't they call his bluff and shoot him right out of the saddle? Blow him to kingdom come?

Suddenly Whipper Smith is terrified. Inside himself he gets down on his knees and prays:

"Lord, tell me what to do when that sedan comes! Here's all these fine good folks, my friends and neighbors, watching me, and they've made me the Peace Officer to protect 'em and now my time's come, the time to do what I was hired for and all dressed up for and I swear, I don't have a diddley-darn of an idea what to do and also I'm so scared that if I don't hold on to this handle bar for dear life I'll fall off this machine flat on my face 'cause I'm too old to cry and too young to die and besides, I don't want to, I want to live a long time and get married to some nice girl and have kids of my own and raise 'em right so they'll be a comfort to me in my old age! The truth is, I've never shot at anybody before, but I will if I have to but I'm prob'ly not a good shooter, I'm so nervous I prob'ly couldn't hit a bull in the behind with a bushel basket! Which reminds me, Lord, speaking of bulls, I beg your pardon for putting that heifer up in your steeple when I was a youngster—I hope you're not mad because I meant no harm or disrespect to You or the Methodists. But I need help now, Lord, I need help something awful, and if You love these folks and this town half as much as I do, please, please tell me what to do!"

Whipper takes out his watch. Two minutes. In two minutes that great green Cadillac V-16 will be here.

Over his shoulder he squints down the highway to the west, toward the city. Nothing.

He unsnaps his holster, draws his pistol. A .38-caliber Smith & Wesson, it glitters. He checks the cartridge clip again and replaces the pistol, leaving the holster flap unsnapped.

To keep himself company, he tries to whistle

a merry tune, "I Wish I Could Shimmy Like My Sister Kate." But his lips fail him. He can't even keep a proper pucker.

He peers down Main Street again. Nothing moves. If the bullets fly, if the air is full of hot lead soon, no one will be killed or wounded. No one else, that is.

One minute now. Whipper Smith sits on the black and silver Harley-Davidson. He can't seem to get enough breath into his lungs. The silence chokes him.

He hears his exhaust pipe, puttering.

His watch, ticking.

The big bass drum of his heart, booming.

One minute.

He sits, waiting.

Waiting.

9. Abadaba

"Smell?" asks Dicksie, her fears confirmed. "We smell?"

"You certainly do," answers Diane Estelle Devere. "You emit the most odorous odor it has ever been the misfortune of my nostrils to encounter. In fact, if I were not too well-brought-up and ladylike to use such an expression, I should say that you stink."

"We're very sorry," Dicksie says. "We didn't know."

"Well, now you do," says the princess. "So please step back."

Still holding hands, brother and sister withdraw a few paces, at which the fair creature returns to her hammock, lies down, arranges her golden curls neatly on the pillow, smoothes her dress, and sips delicately from her glass.

"Whatcha drinkin'?" Auston inquires again.

"Pink lemonade," is the reply. "Are you thirsty?"

"You ain't just bashin' your gums!"

"Then I advise you to go home and have a servant prepare you a glass. There's nothing sweeter than pink lemonade sipped in the shade. Unless it's a cherry phosphate."

"Ever try clam sweat?"

"Clam what? Mercy, you mean perspiration?"

"Naw, sweat," says Auston. "Jab a knife in the shell

an' the clam sweats t'stay closed an' you hold 'im up an' open your trap an' " –he tips his head back, opens his mouth wide, and sticks out his tongue– "slurp, slurp. Nothin' sweeter'n clam sweat, you bet!"

"Oh!" gasps Diane Estelle Devere. "Oh, I shall absolutely perish!"

"Auston, you hush," orders his sister. To make amends, she pays a compliment. "My, that's a pretty dress you're wearing."

"Of course," says Miss Devere.

"Do you mind my asking where you got it?"

"I really don't know. My father purchased it."

"What's your old man do?" asks Auston. "Sell apples?"

"Well, I never!" sniffs the princess. "He's very rich, I'll have you know. I guess we're the only ones in town who aren't poor. We're very sympathetic, however. We often sit around in the evening, my father and mother and I, listening to the radio and eating bonbons, and one of us will say, 'I wonder what the poor are doing tonight?' "

"Bushwah."

"Abadaba," retorts Miss Devere.

"Abadaba!" Auston chortles. He's found a wonderful new word. "Abadaba, abadaba!" he chants.

"I'm looking for the school," says Dicksie, changing the subject.

Diane lifts a limp hand. "Just stroll on to Main Street and turn right one block. Why the school, pray tell?"

"To enroll my brother. He's never been."

"Obviously."

Dicksie will do anything to keep the conversation going, perhaps to make a friend. "Do you go to school?"

"Of course. But I'm staying home today. I have a ripping headache."

"Oh-oh." Auston nudges his sister in the ribs. "Poppa was right–her brain's swole."

The lovely creature looks at Auston. Her lips curl, and then, as though it is too much effort to sneer in the first place, and these visitors are not worth a sneer in the second place, she closes her eyes. Letting down one shoe, she gives a delicate push, and the hammock swings to and fro between the trees, delicately. There is a long, awkward pause, during which, for practice, Auston wiggles all ten toes one at a time. His sister is unhappy. She stands on one boot, then the other. She has one more question to ask before they leave, and finally she says, "Do you think they'll take him? At school, I mean?"

Delicate Diane Estelle Devere's eyebrows raise. "Him? Never."

"Why not?"

"Because he's dirty and smelly and rude and crude and undoubtedly infested with fleas and flies and lice and mice and bugs and slugs and nits and zits, that's why."

Auston glares. "Same to you," he says, "an' many of 'em." He spits expertly over the hammock, ptooey.

Outraged, the princess sits up and stamps a haughty foot. "Which is true of both of you," she says. "I have actually never seen such unwashed, unkempt, underprivileged children as you. In such outlandish attire. I understand we are in the midst of a Depression, but you are inexcusable." She notices something. Her nose wrinkles delicately. Out whisks her handkerchief. "Oh, you've come closer—I shall be desperately ill! Please go! Go!"

Her gray eyes brimming, Dicksie turns and drags her brother after her. For a time they clomp along without a word.

"What a snooty snob," says Auston at length. "I thought you said if I was a gent, folks'd be nice to us."

Dicksie sighs. "We just met her. You mustn't judge a book by its cover."

"I got to, I can't read."

"Besides, I told you not to spit or do your toes or sass, but you did."

"Abadaba."

They pass house after house now, and now a gasoline station, and now a store.

They enter Main Street.

10. Jeepers creepers—here it comes!

Waiting.

His head turned over his shoulder down the highway to the west, gazing.

Peace Officer Whipper Smith's decided what to do, decided because he can't think of anything else. He'll bluff the bank robbers, or try to. He'll sit tight till the sedan passes him, then ride alongside, pull his pistol and aim it into the vehicle and shout "Stop or I'll shoot!" And maybe, just maybe, they'll be so dumbfounded by his daring and gumption that they will.

He tenses. A speck. Becoming a dot. Becoming an automobile. Growing and growing. Faster and faster. Great and green and gruesome.

Jeepers creepers—here it comes!

"This is a town?" Auston demands. They stand at the other end of Main Street, looking about them doubtfully. "You sure it ain't a Pretend Town?"

"Isn't," Dicksie corrects.

They see stores and parked cars but not a single solitary soul except each other. There's no sound, no movement, nothing.

"I thought you said lots of excitin' things goes on in towns," Auston reminds her.

"I did. They do. Let's walk along," she suggests, "and maybe something exciting will happen."

Hand in hand they set out, and since they have never used a sidewalk before, and since the whole empty Main Street is all theirs to take, naturally they start down the middle, the very middle of the highway.

Closer and closer comes the car. Whipper Smith can make out the letters V-16 across the radiator grill, and inside, the heads of three men. He grips the throttle on the handle bars, gets ready.

"Golly," exclaims Dicksie, "golly, look at that. Auston, do you know what that is?"

They stop in the middle of the street.

"I'll bite," says Auston.

"That's a real, honest-to-goodness movie theayter."

They gaup at the name in lightbulbs over the theater: BIJOU. And at the name of the star and the title of the picture playing: CHARLIE CHAPLIN IN "CITY LIGHTS." They goggle at the cardboard pictures of scenes from the film displayed in frames at both sides of the theater.

Ready, hunched over his Harley-Davidson, Peace Officer Smith hears the hum of the sixteen cylinders as the sedan enters town. To make certain everyone is safely inside, out of danger, he takes a last look down Main Street.

Holy Milk of Magnesia! He breaks out in goose bumps. Two stupid little kids standing smack-dab in the middle of the street!

"I can't read it," Dicksie admits, "but I know from the pictures. That's Charlie Chaplin—the funny little man with the derby hat and baggy pants and cane."

"I know it," says Auston. "He was in the last movie magazine we hooked."

Whipper Smith has turned to stone. Behind him, tires hiss on pavement as the Cadillac approaches. But it's slowing down. Do the gangsters note the deserted Main Street? Do they suspect a trap?

"How d'you get in to a movie?" Auston inquires. "Sneak?"

"You do not," his sister responds. "See that booth in the center, like a glass box? Someone sits in there and you give them your money through a hole and they give you a ticket. I think."

What in the name of Heaven will he do now? If he doesn't get those kids out of the middle of the street, the robbers will surely run them down! And if he tries to rescue the kids, they may shoot him down! What's his first duty as a Peace Officer—to stop the thugs or save the children?

"How much money?" asks Auston, who's as full of questions as Zip usually is of beer.

"Ten cents I think. For kids."

"Ten whole cents?" Auston can't believe her. Neither he nor his sister have had as much as a penny of their own to spend. "What a gyp," he snorts.

Whipper Smith twists the throttle. Peeling rubber from his rear wheel he tears away from the curb and heads down the middle of Main Street! Not behind the sedan, but ahead of it! To the people of the town, crowded behind windows, it appears that instead of pursuing the bank robbers, they're pursuing him! Faster and faster, he speeds, and now the people,

who've been watching their Peace Officer, notice the children, and begin to shout at them to look out, to get out of the way!

Poor Dicksie! Poor Auston! They can't budge—they're petrified! Because bearing down on them is a man on a big black and silver motorcycle and right behind him follows a huge automobile and all about them, ringing in their ears over the blast of the motorcycle and the roar of the car are the shouts of strangers! They can't move a muscle! Eyes bulging, they stand helpless, about to be mashed flatter than a pancake by both machines when suddenly—swoop!

A strong arm seizes!

Up they fly on a Ferris wheel!

Away they go on a roller coaster!

Around the corner skids the motorcyle, bounces over the curb, bangs into the brick wall of a grocery store!

Over slams the machine, down the children drop, up leaps Whipper Smith!

At the corner the Cadillac brakes, slows!

"Halt!" shouts the Peace Officer, yanking his pistol and pointing!

He fires at the tires! Once—he misses by a mile! Twice—he slays a watermelon on a stand across the street!

But not again. Something turns the young man's face white as a sheet.

Behind the store windows along Main Street, the townfolk gasp and clutch each other in horror.

For out of the rear window of the great green Cadillac V-16, something is thrust—slowly, slowly—and is aimed at Whipper Smith. A blue-black snout, a muzzle ugly as an insult.

He flings himself to the sidewalk! With one blow he knocks the children down beside him!

The Thompson submachine gun laughs!

11. Hah hah hah hah hah hah hah

On the hollow stage of that Main Street, in the silence of that small, simple town, the sound of the submachine gun is shocking. It is not a cough, not a chatter. To the men, it is mockery. To the women, it resembles an evil sewing machine. From the needle, red flame flickers. A thread of burning lead stitches the air. Slugs slam into the wall of the grocery store over the bodies of Whipper Smith and Dicksie and Auston. Bullets split brick. They scream away into the sky.

Then the laughter ceases. The submachine gun is withdrawn. The great green Cadillac V-16 lurches forward, regains its speed and hurtles out of the town.

Only the echo of the laughter stays, hot and awful in the silence, a curse upon the morning. Listen, the echo seems to say. Never play games again, small town. Never send out a boy upon a bicycle where even grown men dare not go. Find me funny in your fancy, if you wish, and snicker with my snicker on the silver screen–laugh with, but never at me. For I am not the popping of a toy, a strange sound within a story. Hear me in your blood, small town, the echo of the submachine gun whispers, and remember. I was real. I was truth. I was Death.

It is over. The most spine-tingling, heart-stopping moment in the history of the town has passed.

Pale as a ghost, trembling like a leaf after a storm, Peace Officer Whipper Smith rises from the sidewalk by the grocery store.

"Gosh!" he gulps. "Gosh-all-fishhooks! I didn't think they'd have a tommy gun!"

He is utterly discombobulated. His narrow escape has scared him almost out of his socks. He doesn't know what to do, or if he should do anything. He takes off his hat—brushes brick from the brim—puts it on again—takes it off and scratches his head—puts the hat on again—remembers his Harley-Davidson—examines it to see what damage was done by collision with the wall—stands it upright by the curb—remembers the children whose lives he has saved—finds them still lying on the sidewalk where he knocked them down—is frightened a second time by what almost happened to them and to him—becomes furious because he's frightened a second time—grabs brother and sister by an arm—hauls them up like sacks of flour—sits sidesaddle on the motorcycle and spreads his legs—bends the girl over one knee, the boy over the other—and begins to spank the daylights out of them!

"Doggone you kids!" he cries. "I had the street cleared! Wasn't for you standing in the middle of it waiting for a streetcar, I'd have captured those crooks!"

"Ow!" bawls Auston at each spank. He's accustomed to cracks and whacks and bumps and thumps and bangs and whangs about the head, but a plain, ordinary spanking, which hurts his pride more than anything else, seems to him undignified. "Ow!" he protests.

Dicksie will not weep.

But Auston's ow's, a new sound in town, have released it from the safety of the stores and gas stations. People rush into Main Street expecting to find their Peace Officer and the two children blown to bits by bullets. Men and women and babies and aunts and uncles and cousins by the dozens stream from stores and pour around the corner of the grocery and stop short in surprise, then crowd about Whipper and his knee-benders.

"Hey, Whipper, how come you spankin' them kids?" someone wants to know.

"Ow!"

"Hadn't been for them," someone else advises, "you'd be as full of holes as a sieve!"

"Ow!"

Whipper blinks. "What?"

"Ow!"

"Why, those kids savèd your hide!"

Whipper shakes his head. "They did?"

"Ow!"

"Sure they did!"

The young man's baby-blue eyes soften with understanding. He lets his gauntlet gloves rest gently on the backsides of his victims. "That's right," he says. "By the great horn spoon, they did! I saved 'em but they saved me!"

Jerking the children to their feet, he stands over them. "Now, you little dickens," he says, "what were you two doing in the middle of that street?"

Everyone waits. But the children clam up, will not, or cannot, utter a word. That they must not speak to strangers has been beaten into them, after all, and here they stand surrounded by strangers, by more people than they knew existed. But more than that, what would you say, what could you say if, in the last ten minutes, you'd been snubbed by a princess in a pink dress, almost run over by a motorcycle and a sedan, swooped up by an arm, skidded around a corner, smacked into a wall, knocked down, shot at by a submachine gun, jerked and bent over a knee and had the daylights spanked out of you?

All at once, a number of noses start to sniff, and then to wrinkle, and little by little, sniffing and wrinkling, the crowd draws back and spreads for fresh air. Everyone stares at the girl with her mousy hair and her lace-curtain dress, at the boy with bare toes sticking out of rubber boots.

"Haven't I seen you two before?" Whipper Smith demands. "Haven't I? What's your name?"

No answer. His own nose twitches. "You hear me? I said, what's your name?"

Auston's mad. On his chest, the GRO-CHICK grows. He makes fists. "Puddin' Tame," he says defiantly, "ask me again an' I'll tell you the same."

"I know their name." It's a new voice, that of delicate Diane Estelle Devere. Hearing the shots, she has run downtown, but despite the exercise she seems as delicate as ever. "Their names are Dicksie and Auston," she says.

"Dicksie and Auston what?" someone asks.

"Stinker," she replies, pressing her wispy handkerchief to her nostrils.

Everyone hoots. But Whipper Smith draws himself up to his full, manly height and fairly bowls the children over. "Dagnabbit, say something!" he shouts at Dicksie, since she is the elder.

She looks at him adoringly. She clasps her hands. "I love you," she says.

The crowd roars.

Peace Officer Smith blushes red as a beet. His heart is in the right place, but he's absolutely befuddled about the rest of him. Either he's been made a fool of by these smelly little squirts or by those city slickers and their submachine gun. And he can't stand around here all day with his bare, embarrassed face hanging out in public. He must do something, anything! He glances this way–glances that way–cries, "What the diddly-darn am I doing here? I gotta go get those gangsters!"–pulls his pistol–shoves it back–pushes people aside–marches to his Harley-Davidson–leaps upon it–backwards–blushes pink as a petunia and says, "Oops!"–swings himself right-end-to–kicks the starter –grabs the handle bars–throttles the machine up to a fare-thee-well and a cloud of smoke–sets the siren shrieking and guns away like sixty!

The crowd watches him out of sight, then turns around to stare again at the Stinker children. But they are gone.

12. The black valise

With her oars, Dicksie backwaters the button boat. One of the clamming lines is taut. "Got one," she says.

Her brother reaches and, grasping the line, hauls it hand over hand. "Heavy," he says. "Mebbe it's a gold brick."

The catch turns out to be a galosh laden with mud and water. Auston unhooks it and lets it burble downward into the river.

He snorts. Two hours later, he's still madder than a hornet. "If that's what towns is like," he declares, "I'm never goin' in one of 'em again."

"Are like," his sister corrects.

"Dry up an' blow away!" he snarls. "Whatta you get, goin' into a town? Snooted by some stuck-up girl an' shot at by bank robbers an' laughed at by folks—an' if it's a lickin' I want, I can get licked right here t'home!"

Dicksie sighs. Auston's in a very sassy mood this afternoon, and for once she cannot blame him. Her attempt to introduce them to the world and to enroll him in school has backfired, and for reasons she herself had never expected. How will she ever persuade him to believe her again? How can she argue successfully if he refuses even to go to Pretend School?

They float along quietly for a time. The only lucky thing about this day, she thinks, is that they were safely back at the shack when Jake returned at noon from clamming. Had he suspected where they'd been, he might have yanked them baldheaded. But he had heard a siren along the highway beyond the woods—several sirens in fact—and curious to learn what the racket was all about, and always glad for an excuse to wet his whistle with beer, he went himself into town, taking Zip and ordering the children to replace him in the boat.

Dicksie lifts the oars. From the blades, water drip-drip-drips like tears. Shadow falls. They drift under the highway bridge beside which, only yesterday, a young man tall and slim and handsome sat upon his noble motorcycle. The young man whose life they might have saved by standing stupidly in the middle of Main Street. Whose thanks had been a public spanking. Gazing at the bridge, she scarcely notices when Auston clambers over her seat to the opposite end of the button boat to raise another line. Remembering, she doesn't notice that, trying to haul up the taut line, he huffs and puffs with effort.

"Dicks."

She rouses. "What?"

"Help me. This ain't no clam—I got a whale."

She turns and, getting down beside him on her knees in the scummy bottom, heaves away carefully so that the line won't break. Up, up it comes, and suddenly, out of the dark water appears a handle. Both get a grip on it, and together they lift something black and leather and streaming water into the scow. Two straps are buckled over the top.

"I give up," says Auston.

"It's a valise."

"What's that?"

"Like a suitcase, only smaller. To carry clothes and things in when you're traveling."

"Just what I need," he snorts. "Well, lessee." Unbuckling the straps, he pushes a catch and spreads the top wide. "Mebbe it's fulla money." They peer inside.

It is.

13. Dicksie's dream

It is! The valise is chock-full of money!

On their knees, brother and sister stare at stack upon stack of soggy paper money, each green stack bound neatly by a strip of paper.

Suppose you have never had a penny of your own to save or spend. A stranger to coins, the sight of paper money in large quantities doesn't at first excite you in the least. You simply do not believe it's real. And during a Depression, it can't be.

Auston takes out a stack. "These dollar bills?"

So does Dicksie. "No."

"How come?"

"Because dollar bills have number one in the corners."

He examines his stack. "Mine've got a one an' two doughnuts."

"So've mine. They're not doughnuts, they're nothings."

"You mean we hooked a bagful of nothin's?"

"A number one and two nothings means a hundred."

"A hunderd," he repeats.

"See if yours are all alike. Mine are."

He separates the corners of his stack. "Yup." He looks at his sister. "A hunderd," he says. "I don't know what that means an' you know I don't."

"They're hundred-dollar bills. Each one is worth one hundred dollars."

But he still doesn't understand a hundred, and like a good teacher, she searches for an example. "Last year that's how much Poppa got for all his clamshells. Five of these."

"Oh," he says. "How much you reckon's in here?"

His sister pokes about in the valise. "Some are 5's and nothings, that's fifty dollars. Some are 1's and nothings, that's ten."

"How much?"

"I don't know. Thousands, though."

"Thousan's," he repeats. She might as well have said pounds or peaches or doodlebugs. "Is that rich?"

"Very rich."

"Really very rich?"

"Really. Very."

Kneeling in the bottom of the button boat, the black valise between them, through the sleepy afternoon they glide. Unattended, the oars bump against the sides of the scow. From high in a tree on the bank, a crow caws at them. A turtle surfaces nearby, watching them, its flippers waving.

Suddenly Auston jumps up and inflates his GRO-CHICK and opens his mouth and out of him rises a shout that makes the crow fly and the turtle dive and the very river ring:

"Rich!" he shouts. "Rich, rich, I'm rich as a witch! Lord, Lord, I'm as rich as Ford!"

His words are crushed. Dicksie, too, leaps to her feet and throws her arms about him so tightly that his joy is lost in lace curtain. "Auston, Auston, what if Poppa hears you!"

Her fear penetrates him. He hugs her back, and they sway together awkwardly, almost toppling over the side—for both children understand her meaning far better than riches. "Dicks, what'll we do?" Auston wails. "What'll we do?"

"I don't know, I have to think." She releases him. "We have to hide it, somewhere near us, and starting right this minute." Up and down the stream she looks, then kneeling again, quickly snaps the valise shut and buckles the straps. With his help, she wedges it under the covered top of his end of the scow. "Sit in front of it," she orders, "on the bottom." She returns to the seat and takes the oars again. "Now we'll clam as though nothing's happened. We can talk about it on the way home, but no one can see what's behind you."

Along they float, each busy with his thoughts, pretending to watch the lines as usual, Auston with his back smack against the square-ended, covered top, Dicksie keeping their course steady, her back to her brother. At first their fright lingers. "It's ours, ain't it, Dicks?" Auston whispers. "Finders keepers?"

"Isn't it. Yes, finders keepers. I don't say he'd take it if he guessed, but he might. We must try to think the best of everyone, Auston, but Poppa is weak."

"Weak abadaba. He's a no-count drunk."

In time, as they feel more secure with their secret, the importance of the black valise sinks into them. It is a miracle. At age eleven and age nine, their life may be completely changed if they wish. Everything in fact is different now. To the tongue, the air of afternoon is tart as apple cider. Altered by autumn, the trees along the river bend low to girl and boy in graceful bows of red and gold.

"Rich," gloats Auston. He makes his voice delicate and snobby. "We're very rich," he mimics. "We often sit around, my sister'n me, listenin' t'the radio an' eatin' bonbons an' spittin' under the rug an' one of us'll say, 'I wonder what them poor folks is doin' t'night.' "

Dicksie smiles in spite of herself.

"We go dibs on the moolah, don't we, Dicks? Half mine'n half yours?"

"We'll see?"

"Well, I already know what I'm gonna do with mine."

"What?"

Since her back is to him, Auston fishes from a pocket of his raggedy pants a cigarette and a wooden match. The cigarette he's homemade himself, of Indian tobacco twisted into a scrap of old newspaper. Scratching the match against the scow side, he lights the weed, leans back and crosses his boots and puffs and blows a cloud of proud smoke. "Well, I'm movin' outa the shack an' buildin' me a better one an' buyin' a button boat an' a motorcycle an' a barrel of beer. I'll clam if I want to, an' if I don't, I'll ride on my motorcycle t'town an' laugh at people. But mostly I'll jus' set around livin' the life of Riley an' count my money an' gargle with beer an'–"

"Auston!"

The cloud has reached his sister. Turning to see if the button boat is on fire, she shoots to her boots.

"Smoking! You little snip!" Coughing, she stumbles over the seat, snatches the cigarette from his fingers, and flings it into the water. "How dare you!" she cries, bending over him.

Auston tries to declare that he dares because he's rich, but his throat is full of smoke and besides, the rage on Dicksie's face warns him to cough instead, which he needs to do anyway. When an older sister has a hissy, younger brothers do well to wait it out.

"Oh, Auston!" Dicksie's gray eyes fill, but she will not weep. "If I don't reform you before it's too late, you'll be just like Poppa!"

"Tattooed?" Auston inquires.

"Oh!" Shaking her head, she collapses onto the seat in a heap of lace curtain and misery. For a while she sits with chin propped in her hands, staring a hole right through her brother, pondering her many problems. The button boat drifts this way and that, the lines loosening, tightening, snarling. Keeping mum, Auston hooks a clam and waits. And finally, as they near the shack, his sister folds her hands and announces her decision.

"Auston," she says, "I have made up my mind. I have decided what we'll do with the money. I'm responsible for you and I simply will not 'low you to waste your half on loose living. So we'll spend it together, for something worthwhile."

Auston scowls.

"We are going to run away," Dicksie continues. "We'll hide the valise close by, and soon's we can, we'll take Zip and run away down-river somewheres, to some nice little town. We'll buy a darling white cottage with a radio and running water and a flower garden and inside toilets." Her tone softens. "We'll live happily ever after in our house, just the three of us. I'll cook and clean. Zip will dry out and learn to like water and milk. Every night we'll go to the movie theayter—Zip will have no fleas and guard the house. And every day, dear brother, you will go to school." She smiles. "There, doesn't that sound nice, Auston?"

He looks at her.

"Doesn't it sound heavenly?" She smiles a sisterly-motherly-auntly-heavenly smile.

Auston looks at her. "Pardon me," he says, "while I puke."

"Auston, you hush!" Dicksie glares at him, then heaves a sigh of mingled anger and despair, a masterpiece of a sigh, which whooshes like a windstorm all the way up from her rubber boots. When she can calm herself, she presses her lips together in a firm, determined line. "I am ashamed," she says, "of my very own brother. Would you care to know why?"

"I'm gonna," he grumbles, "whether I w'nta or not."

"Yes, you are. I'm ashamed because you've forgotten."

"Forgotten?"

"Her."

Once again, instantly, the word works its magic. "Oh." Sheepishly the boy lowers his head.

"Auston, I've had a dream for years and years—it was Her dream, and all She had to leave us. That one day we'd get away from the river and this boat and clams and the shack and beer and smells and live clean and decent like most folks. It's what She dreamed and prayed for—why, it's almost like She dropped that valise in the river for us to hook. It's Her gift to us." Dicksie stands and lifts her head bravely. "So stand up, Auston, and say 'I promise Her.'"

Before the force of these words, before the memory of a mother he can scarcely remember, Auston has no choice. He hesitates. "School every day?"

"Every day. But a movie every night. Mae West, Laurel and Hardy and Hoot Gibson and W. C. Fields and Greta Garbo and George Raft and popcorn."

"Popcorn? I promise," he swears, but behind his back, his fingers are crossed.

"Her," his sister adds.

Auston uncrosses his fingers. "Okey-doke, Her."

They clam home. After making sure the coast is clear, they scamper the black valise ashore and bury it deep within the clamshell pile, the same pile under which they hid themselves from Whipper Smith the day before. Then, as though nothing whatever has happened except the weather, they plump themselves onto the pile and begin to clean the afternoon's catch. They're lucky a second time, for in less than two jerks of a lamb's tail, down the snake-track road through the woods into the cove, staggering and weaving, come Jake and Zip.

"Poor Poppa. Poor Zip," sighs Dicksie.

"Poor horsefeathers," says Auston. "Drunk as skunks."

14. Jake's dream

That night they feast. Besides a bellyful of beer for himself and Zip, Jake has splurged twenty cents on two pounds of chicken necks and a loaf of bread. Dicksie boils the necks until, bubbling in good, thick, muddy river water, she has a good, thick, muddy broth. Now they sit around the table and around Zip, who snores and scratches in the center, and they dine, gnawing at the necks and dipping whole slices of bread in the broth. Dicksie nibbles. Auston squinches his eyes shut. He hates chicken necks, and these must have come, he's certain, from the skinniest, toughest old biddies in the coop. Their stepfather, however, gobbles with gusto. The broth spatters. And when he cannot easily separate the meat from the tiny bones with his teeth, he stuffs the entire neck into his mouth and crunches it up like a sausage grinder, swallowing bones and all. What is even more interesting, he manages to talk a blue streak, even with his mouth crammed.

He's telling the children all the news he learned at the poolroom in town this afternoon–about the bank robbers comin' through an' that Keystone Kop of a Whipper Smith clearin' Main Street an' schemin' t'stop 'em but bein' the town joke instead because two knothead kids was standin' in the middle of the street an', instead of shootin' it out with the crooks,

God Bless
our
Happy Home

Whipper took a notion t'rescue the kids—nobody ever found out who they was—an' the gangsters got away scot free. But not far, because a mile or so outa town the State Police, called in their cars by radio, chased an' caught 'em an' now they was safely under lock an' key in the big city clink. How he wishes he'd of saw the whole Our Gang comedy! How he wishes he'd of saw the look on Peace Ossifer Smith's phiz when that submachine gun started playin' a tune on that brick pianna!

"But that ain't the best part." Jake grabs the last slice of bread from the wrapper, sloshes it in broth, bites off half, and points the other half at his hairy chest. "See ol' Lucky Lindy here? Well, he wasn't —not compared t'your dear daddy. Your dear daddy's 'bout t'be a rich man." He finishes off the bread, leans back in his chair, and wipes his mouth with a bare arm. "Yup, rich. An' when I am, I'm buildin' a better house for us an' buyin' me a motorcycle—gettin' too far for me t'walk t'town—an' a hull barrel of beer. You kids'll do the clammin', it's good for you t'be out'n the fresh air'n sunshine. As for me, when I get tuckered out countin' my money, I'll ride my machine t'town an' have the last laugh on them stuck-up town folks."

Dicksie and Auston look at each other.

Jake pauses to pick his teeth with a finger. "Don't b'lieve me, do you? Well, you bend your lazy ears. Them robbers stole six thousan' dollars from that city bank—an' you know where that loot's at now? Right close by!"

Auston and Dicksie look at each other.

Jake tips forward and bumps his elbows down on the table, waking Zip, who burps. "Right close by! I figger right by the road t'other side of our woods—an' tomorrow mornin' I'll be out lookin' for it! Hull town'll be out too—there's a ree-ward of one hunderd dollars for whosomever finds it—but I say finders keepers!"

He grins at his audience and blows a little broth. "Six thousan' simoleons jus' layin' aroun' for your dear daddy t'lay hands on! B'cause when them crooks was bein' chased in their car by the State Police, they didn't want t'be caught with the goods, now did they? So you know what? They throwed it out the windy!"

Brother and sister gulp.

"Say, what's wrong with you two?"

They seem to be choking on chicken necks.

15. Every day in every way I'm getting better and better

Will he never, never go?

They nearly bust with waiting while Jake wakes in the morning and yawns and stretches and grunts and groans and has three cups of coffee and finally, finally, telling them to clam while he's gone, leaves with Zip to search the sides of the highway for the six thousand dollars.

The second he's out of sight, Dicksie and Auston dive into the clamshell pile to dig up the black valise.

"What'll we do with it?" Auston pants.

"Mercy, I don't know," his sister admits, "but we can't keep it here—'right close by' he said! We have to hide it somewhere else while I think what to do—I know, Pretend School!"

To the button boat they hustle the valise. Together, each splashing an oar, they row to the landing in the woods. Through the trees they trot, into the surprise glade lovely with sunlight, noisy with birds, and busy with bugs. Nothing has changed here—the cardboard desk, the latest movie magazine fished from the river, dried now, the vase of ferns, wilted now, the rows of bottle boys and girls waiting patiently for Reading Class to begin. Down they flop to catch their breath.

"Lessee if it's still in here," Auston says, unbuckling the straps and opening the bag. "Hot spit!" he chortles. "Oh, you hot mazuma! Six thousan' dollars!" He removes a stack of soggy bills and plays catch with it, tossing it high in the air over his head. He's never seen a baseball game, but Jake has described the sport. "Fly ball t'lef' field–Babe Ruth moves to his right, holds out his mitt–wump! A long out!" He grins at his sister. "Hey, Miss Rockerfeller, watch the ol' ball game." But his sister is silent, seated in a position he knows and dreads, her thinking position, chin in hands. "Dollar for your thoughts, Dicks," he says. "I'm a big spender now."

Dicksie sighs. "Auston, we have to give it back."

"Come again?"

"We have to give the money back."

He sticks a finger in his ear. "Must have somethin' in here. Come again?"

"Auston, you heard me."

"Give it back!" His outcry slashes through the trees. He jumps up and stomps in pain between the rows of pupils. "Whatta you talkin' about? Finders keepers!"

Sadly but surely she explains. It is plain as the nose on her face what happened yesterday. During the chase by the State Police, the crooks in the great green Cadillac V-16 threw the black bag out the window while racing across the highway bridge over the river. It sank. They hooked it. Finders keepers was a proper policy so long as they didn't know whose it was or how to return it, but now they knew. It belongs to a bank in the big city, and it is therefore their duty, hers and his, to hand it over to its rightful owners.

"A bank! Who gives a whoodly-squat about a bank!" Auston rages. "Who needs it more'n us? Do banks like t'go t'movies? Do they catch clams an' eat chicken necks? Who ever heard of a poor bank?"

Dicksie waits adultly for the tantrum to pass, then proceeds. There are indeed banks badly off now—there's a terrible Depression throughout the United States. Both of them have heard Poppa tell how only last year every bank in the country was closed for a spell, by order of President Roosevelt. And besides, banks just keep people's money safe for them. Probably this six thousand dollars really belongs to widows and orphans, who'll be lonely and hungry till it's returned to them.

"I'm lonely!" Auston bawls. "I'm hungry!"

And also honest, his sister adds, honest enough to do the right thing—and he knows in his heart that if they keep money, which truly isn't theirs, they are just as robbery as the bank robbers.

Auston stops stomping up and down and scowls at her. "Okay, okay, what're we gonna do?"

"I've been thinking about that too. We can't hike into town, we might meet Poppa. So we'll spread the money out to dry tonight, right here, the way we do magazines and, first thing tomorrow morning, we'll sneak over here, gather it up and take it into town and give it to that Peace Officer."

"Yaaaah!" Auston sneers. "I thought so! You just want t'see Whipper Smith again—you're stuck on him like flypaper! Stuck!"

Dicksie blushes. "That's not the reason and you know it." Quickly she changes the subject. "Anyways, Auston," she reminds him, "we'll get a hundred-dollar reward."

"Bushwah we will. Poppa'll take it away from us so fast our heads'll swim an' you know that!"

"Then our reward," says his sister primly, "will be a clear conscience."

"Oh yeah? You take your conscious—gimme popcorn!" Giving up, Auston waves his arms in disgust with all women. Running to the valise, he sits down and sweeps it into his arms, cuddling it like a child. "Oh, I can't stand it!" he wails. "All this beeyootiful cabbage—I'll die!"

"She did, Auston."

The boy opens his mouth as though to protest, then closes it as Dicksie continues. "But before She did, She told me something. She said school and clothes and manners are important, but not as much as something else. Char'cter. Char'cter, Auston. Which you can't buy, you have to earn."

To her surprise, even to his, Auston sighs. "Well, I'll sure have plenty—six thousan' bucks worth." Bitterly he puts the black bag down. "Mebbe I'll go on all my life rowin' a button boat an' eatin' garbage an' gettin' beat on, but I'll smell of char'cter stronger'n I do of clams."

Dicksie smiles. "I know, dear brother. There goes our cottage and garden and school and movies, Her dream for us and mine too. But every cloud has a silver lining, remember that. Do you know what else

She said? She said if when you're unhappy and low-down, if you just close your eyes and say to yourself over and over one thing, it'll help: 'Every day in every way I'm getting better and better.' Just say it over and over and sure enough, things will get better."

But Auston mopes. Finding a bug on his ear, he mashes it to a pulp. And becoming the good teacher again, to take his mind off his sacrifice Dicksie busies them both by opening the black valise and removing, one by one, the stacks of soaked currency in their paper bands. In order to dry them overnight, her idea is to divide each stack into two thinner ones, then curl up each thinner stack and twist it into the top of a beer bottle like a cork. With this method, none of it will blow away and air will dry it fully. Back and forth along the rows they go, until every bottle boy and girl has a curl of currency for a cap, until the valise is empty and they can hide it under a huckleberry bush. Dicksie is pleased that Auston seems willing to assist her in the task. Would she be as pleased if she knew that, as they reach the last row of the Pretend School, and as her back is turned to him, her dear brother slips a dollar bill into his shirt?

16. "God bless our happy home"

His boots off, prepared to pop into bed, Auston stretches.

"Whazzat?" says Jake, pointing.

Auston glances down guiltily at his chest. Yikes! There's a hole in the center of the O in his GRO-CHICK sack shirt! And in the hole, as Jake and Dicksie and Zip and even he, Auston, can clearly see by the light of the kerosene lamp, is something green!

"Whazzat?"

Auston swallows hard. "Green skin, I guess. From eatin' chicken necks."

"Green skin!" growls Jake. "We'll see!" Bursting from his bed, he rams a hand down Auston's shirt front, pulls out a dollar bill. A crisp new dollar bill. "New money," he says, "bank money. Where'd you get it?"

Auston sets a stubborn jaw.

Jake is cantankerous and weary. For hours he's searched up and down along the highway for the robbery loot—harder work than he has done in years—and nothing to show for it but blisters. He towers over his stepson like a tree. "I'm gonna ask you for the las' time, boy. You found that six thousan' somewhere, didn't you? That's bank money—the only where's you can get yourself a bran' new dollar. You found it an' you let me walk my legs off lookin'. The las' time, boy. Now where's it at?" Jake raises a paw.

Auston closes his eyes against the blow he knows is coming.

But it doesn't. Instead of striking the boy, his usual punishment, he lifts Auston bodily off his feet, raises him high and hurls him across the shack into the pile of iron muskrat traps, which clatter down about him, shaking the very walls of the shack.

"Poppa!" Dicksie screams. "I'm the one! I found the money and I hid it!" Only to protect her brother would she ever, ever fib. "Auston doesn't know where!"

Like a wild bull, Jake turns on her, lumbers toward her. "You! I shoulda knowed! Where's it at? Speak up—where's that money at?"

Dicksie retreats around the stove. "Please, Poppa," she begs. "It isn't ours—I have to give it back!"

"Give it back? I'll give you!" Again Jake raises the club of his grubby hand, then stays it. He stands sweating, thinking. In this gritty, gray-eyed, mouse-haired girl he's met his match. He's bashed her black and blue many a time, and more bumps and lumps will never take the remarkable starch out of her. No, he must try a different tack. Backing off, he sits down on a box and covers his stubbly face with his hands.

"May your dear dead Momma forgive me," he blubbers. "I come nigh t'hittin' you again, my darlin' girl—I'm a beast, a animal, a rotten brute!" How, he pleads, can they be so selfish as to keep secrets from him? After all he's done for them? After all these years? His belly rolls with self-pity. He tries to make them understand what the money means to him. "I'm just a common, no-good button boatman, an' that six thousan'd change my whole life, an' yours too! We'd be somebody! Why, if you was t'tell me where it's at—why, the both of you could go to school! You hear that? School!" Pretending to scoop away a flood of tears, he peeks through his fingers to see what effect his performance is having. "So tell me, please. If you respec' an' love me as I worship the ground you walk on, my babies, you'll tell your dear ol' daddy an' bring joy'n gladness to his achin' heart! Please, pretty please?" he implores. "With sugar on it?"

He drops his hands.

"Poppa," says Dicksie sorrowfully but bravely, "I don't believe a word you say."

With a roar Jake rises, tipping over the whole table, sending Zip yipping under a box. The next minute is the most violent the shack has ever lived through, even worse than the night he threw a beer bottle at his stepdaughter and broke the window. Jake goes on a rampage. Cursing and swearing, he seizes Dicksie, lifts the trap door, and pushes her headlong into the cold pit.

"I'll show you!" he thunders down at the girl. "I'll see how much sand you got, she-cat! You'll stay down there an' eat mud till you starve! I don't give a tinker's darn if you don't see daylight again till you go blind! But starve or blind, you ain't comin' out b'fore you tell me where at that money is!"

Slamming down the trap door with a crash, he

weights it with the chair, then spying Auston, yanks him out of the muskrat traps and throws him across the shack onto his bed. Finally, kicking over a box and uncovering Zip, he kicks the hound in the slats, blows out the lamp and, still cursing and swearing, falls into the filthy skins on his bed.

In the cold pit, Dicksie waits.

For a time Jake scratches and snuffles, so sorry for himself that he cannot sleep. "Six thousan' smackers," he mumbles. "Lazies', lyines', selfishes' brats ever brung into the world."

Dicksie waits. What if Auston, beaten and battered, falls asleep before Poppa? Whatever will she do?

"She was a good woman," Jake grumbles, "but she done me wrong. Leavin' me with such as these t'raise —an' not even mine."

He snores.

In the dark and slime of the cold pit, Dicksie twists herself slowly, slowly into a sitting position, careful not to clink the bottles beneath her. Now she can peer through a split in the wooden trap door, through the legs of the chair weighting it. Enough moonlight enters the broken window so that she can make out certain objects. There is the framed motto on the wall: GOD BLESS OUR HAPPY HOME. She cranes her head, strains her eyes through the black.

There! God bless her dear, bruised brother! There, dangling from a bed, a signal in the moonlight—five dirty toes wiggling, one at a time!

She taps the trap door. In a moment she can hear his breathing over her. Through the split they plot in whispers. She insists there's only one thing to do —he must go now, quietly, go and row the button boat to Pretend School, pack up the money in the valise, then row down-river to town and find Whipper Smith and turn it over to him. Who, he hisses, me? Now? At night? Alone?

A pause. She can almost hear him shake his head.

Then he whispers, unh-unh, he's sorry, he wants to help her, but if she thinks he's goin' into that wild and woolly town by himself, at night, she's nuttier than a fruitcake. Why, he was almost mowed down by a submachine gun in the daytime! No, ma'am, she'd better have another brainstorm!

Dicksie huddles hopelessly. Why, oh why, did he snitch that dollar bill! But she will not weep. She thinks and thinks. Oh, if only she knew how to write! She hears Jake snore. Zip whimpers. He's having a dogmare. Oh, if Auston only knew how to write! She thinks and thinks. Eureka!

"Auston?"

"What?" he whispers through the split.

"Listen–"

17. Lily! Lily! Lily!

He beaches the button boat. Lame, limping, crippled up from being pitched into the pile of muskrat traps, he hobbles up the path through the woods on bare feet. The night is blacker than the ace of spades. He steps on something cold and damp.

A snake!

Darn that Dicksie. Why does he have to have her for a sister? For that matter, what has he done to deserve any sister? He bumps into something.

A bear!

He's scared to his spizzerinctum. Every day in every way he's getting better and better phooey! What's that? Something screeches.

A hant!

He runs–stumbling, tripping, aching, quaking. By the time he lurches into the secret glade, their Pretend School, Auston's a nervous wreck. His skin crawls, his goose bumps are as big as jawbreakers. And even though there's moonlight here, a pale filter falling through the branches of the trees, it's still night and he's still alone and still a nine-year-old boy.

He tries to run but can't. How'll he ever do what Dicksie wants? Pack up the money and bring it back to the shack and bury it again in the clamshell pile before someone dishonest searching in the woods finds it before she gets out of the cold pit? How can

he ever turn the snakes to stone and bamboozle the bears and lay the hants to rest? How?

Then he remembers. With one word?

"Lily?" he whispers. Then louder, "Lily?"

The echo of that word hangs upon the moonbeams, tender and brave, a blessing in the night. Listen, the echo seems to say. I am only a name, small boy, the name of someone long ago and far away. But while

I linger on your lips, while I have a haven in your heart, I am here, and I will keep you from all harm. Remember me, dear small boy. Utter me over and over, the echo whispers, and forget me not, for I am stronger than Death. I am real. I am alive. I am Love.

"Lily! Lily! Lily!" he cries, restored. Dashing to the huckleberry bush, he locates the valise. "Lily!" Up and down the rows of bottle boys and girls he goes, ramming and jamming and cramming handfuls of bills into the bag. "Lily!" The bag filled, he tears down the path from the Pretend School through the woods to the river, the sound of Her name in the night surrounding him with arms that make him noble, swift, and loved. "Lily!"

Upriver he oars the scow like a speed demon, breathing more easily now and, reaching the cove, lets the button boat glide to a landing. He tiptoes to the clamshell pile. One last thing to do—bury the black valise again without waking Jake.

No! He's forgotten what he's supposed to remember! Since he was afraid to go into town alone, and since neither of them could write a note, Dicksie had a flash how to send word to town that the robbery loot has been found so that the townfolk will begin looking for it. Someone, she was sure, will carry the word to Peace Officer Smith, and he will lead the search in person.

Pussyfooting to the beer bottle pile, Auston brings two bottles to the valise and stuffs a bill in each, then takes them to the river bank and throws them as far out into the current as he can. Splash. Splash. In the moonlight the bottles bob, then float away, carrying their messages. Surely one of them will reach town, if not both. Surely one of them, if not both, will fall into the hands of someone who'll understand the meaning of new money as quickly as Jake did, and rush with it to Whipper Smith.

Now he can bury the bag at the edge of the clamshell pile, saying ssssh to himself at every click and clatter. Now he can hold his breath and spider into the shack, around the table and through the snores, can get down on hands and knees under the chair but over the split in the trap door.

"Dicks?" he whispers.

"Yes?"

"I done it!"

"Did it," she corrects. "Was the money there?"

"Yup."

"Did you send the dollar bills in bottles?"

"You ain't just a-woofin'," he brags. "They had ones on 'em, an' two doughnuts."

"Ones and two doughnuts!" she gasps. "Auston, those were hundred-dollar bills! Oh, Auston!"

18. Should a heifer believe everything her mother tells her?

Through the night a beer bottle sails.

It strikes a snag, the branch of a submerged tree, drifts free.

Round and round in an eddy it twirls, rides free.

Hour after hour it bobs and wallows until, in the early morning light, wafted by a wayward wind, it comes to a sandy stop in shallow water by a moss meadow just as a herd of cows comes down to the river to wade and drink and wash before breakfast. One of the herd is a brown and white and innocent heifer. A heifer is a young lady cow who has not yet been out on a date.

Daintily she wades into the water. Sweetly she steps knee-deep into the sand. Thinking of other things, she pays little heed to a beer bottle by her hoof, a bottle with something green inside.

She is thinking about the long talk she had last night with her mother before going to bed. Her mother's advice, it seems to her, makes good horse sense. Beware of boys, her mother began. Boys are often naughty. But meanwhile, her mother went on, contradicting herself, be as attractive as you can at all times. Use your tail to flick flies. Lick your nose with your tongue to keep it shiny. Flick and lick and think pure thoughts.

But the question is, should a heifer believe everything her mother tells her? Her own mother, for example, is fond of telling a story about a situation in which she was personally involved years ago when she was a very young lady. One Halloween, the story goes, she was cownaped from her pasture in the night by a cute but naughty boy and forced up a flight of stairs into a church steeple and tied there until the bells rang and the organ played and the congregation sang and she bawled herself simply sick on Sunday morning! Now this is the craziest, cock-and-bull whopper her daughter has ever heard, and she finds it impossible to believe, which makes her doubt some of the other things her mother tells her.

Licking and flicking and being attractive and pondering the matter, the heifer steps innocently upon the beer bottle, driving it deep under the sand, sinking it forever.

19. A river of cherry phosphates

Through the night the other bottle sails.

Fish blow bubbles at it.

On its glassy, tinkly sides, a water snake plays a tune with its tail.

When the sun is high it approaches the town, gliding toward houses and stores and people. Surely someone soon will see it. Surely someone soon will read its message and hurry it off to Whipper Smith, for half the town's been looking for the loot.

But wait! As it drifts nearer, nearer, it's snagged by the branch of a tree that leans low over the river. Hour after hour the bottle dances with the branch, embraced by leaves, a prisoner by a big brick house standing splendidly in wide lawns and beds of flowers.

In the afternoon, a girl idles along the river after school, a princess with long golden tresses, a fair creature crisp in a dainty yellow dress with ribbons. Chancing to spy the bottle dancing with the branch, delicately she breaks another branch and stretching, fetches the prize from the water.

There's something green inside. Curious, she slips it out, stares. She can scarcely believe what her eyes tell her.

Ooh-la-la! A hundred-dollar bill!

Hastily she glances about to be certain no one has seen her. No one has, no one will ever know.

Innocently she folds and tucks the bill into a pocket and skips across the lawn.

While she adores pink lemonade sipped in the shade, there's something else she adores even more. She simply loves to perch on a stool at the counter in the drugstore and pay her nickel and delicately draw a cherry phosphate through a straw. She smiles, tasting the thousands of cherry phosphates a hundred dollars will buy. Closing her eyes, she imagines a whole river of cherry phosphates delighting her delicate tonsils.

20. Escape!

Is it day? Is it night? In the darkness of the cold pit, Dicksie cannot tell.

Why hasn't Whipper Smith answered her plea for help? What happened to the bottles? How long has she been imprisoned? It seems years.

In the damp, she shivers. Her arms and legs and hair and dress are slippery with slime. She tries to think, to measure time backwardly by event. Last night Poppa put her here and Auston brought the money from the Pretend School and buried it again in the clamshell pile. Yesterday she decided to return it to its rightful owners. The day before that they went into town, met Diane Estelle Devere, were saved from certain death by Whipper Smith, and that afternoon hooked the black valise from the river bottom. The day before that, while clamming, they encountered the new Peace Officer by the highway bridge.

Only three days? Can all these things have happened in only three days or has she miscounted? She's so weak from hunger and thirst that she fears she'll never see another morning. By uncapping and drinking from one of the beer bottles beside her, she could sustain herself, but she has a will of iron and, though tempted, she resists. She knows what beer can do, and she will die, she swears, before she'll foul her lips with strong drink.

Die? She's too young! And too young to be buried alive like this! And if she should die, what should be her grave? The bottom of the river, probably, with heavy stones for flowers. Her eyes brim. Yes, Poppa would coffin her with rocks, and no one but the clams would mourn. But she will not weep.

The clomp of boots and voices over her. Poppa and Auston and Zip are back from clamming. Poppa has caught a fat catfish on his trotline, and proceeds to fry it for supper while Auston cleans the clams. Just before they sit down to eat, the trap door is raised. Jake bends over her.

"What's this? Dear girl, why d'you stay down there by your lonesome? Fish for supper—won'tcha come up an' eat with me'n your brother?" he wheedles. "Just say the word, little darlin', just say where that money's at an' you can fill your tummy."

Dicksie's almost blinded by the lamplight. She shakes her head. "I can't, Poppa. I must do what's right."

Jake spits splat into the cold pit. "Then stay down there!" he roars, his dander up again. "Stay there an' watch us feed our faces an' see how you like it!"

Reaching down, he brings up a bottle of beer and shares it with Zip while man and boy and dog dine on catfish. The smells and the sight of others eating are almost more than Dicksie can bear, and when Jake fingers the fishbones from his mouth and tosses them at her, she turns her head away. But not before she catches Auston's wink.

Supper over, the dishes washed in the bucket, Jake drops the trap door again with a crash and weights it with the chair. "Nighty-night," he taunts his step-daughter. "Sleep tight an' don't let no bugs bite. Come mornin', you might not be so high-falutin'."

The kerosene lamp goes out. She hears them crawl into the beds under the filthy muskrat skins. She waits, listening to Jake grunting and tossing, praying he will soon fall asleep and Auston will stay awake. Finally there are snores, and soon a movement above her.

"Psssst. Dicks?"

She drags herself to the split. "Auston?"

"It ain't the Queen of Sheba."

"Oh, Auston, I'll never live through another night!"

"I saved you a hunk of fish, but that pig of a Zip et it."

"Ate it. Thanks just the same. But I have to get out or I'll be too weak to walk or anything."

"Okay," he whispers, "whadda we do?"

"We're going to escape, both of us, and take the money. I've been thinking. First, go outdoors and dig up the valise and put it in the button boat. Then come back here and move the chair away and raise the trap door just enough for me to climb out. But Auston, you can't make a single sound!"

"You're tellin' me. Okey-doke, stick around."

Again she waits. For hours, it seems. She can hear nothing.

Then the scrape of a chair leg overhead.

The trap door rises. A squeak.

Slowly, painfully, she crawls through the opening. Her hands meet Auston's. Together they lower the trap door. Now for the door.

It's black as a tomb in the shack. Like blind children, their hands before them, feeling, they shuffle toward the door. But Dicksie's been sitting or lying down for a night and a day, and her legs are cramped. She staggers.

A horrible howl!

She's stepped on Zip's tail! Having had too much beer to jump into bed with his master, the drunkard dog has gone to sleep on the floor!

"Whazzat? What the!"

"Run, Auston, run!" cries Dicksie. Through the dark they stumble and bumble, tipping over boxes and traps as Jake charges from the bed! Like the Katzenjammer Kids they squeeze and scramble through the door, their stepfather after them cursing and swearing!

As fast as their legs will carry them they speed for the button boat, push it from the bank, clamber in!

"You stop!" Jake shouts.

Brother and sister grab the same oar, then drop it and both grab the other.

"Stop or I'll kill you!" Jake trumpets.

He dives headfirst into the river after them, drenching them with spray, his arms outstretched for the scow!

One on each oar, the children row with all their might and main!

His fingers touch the button boat!

21. Murder!

And fall away.

For they forge ahead faster now, into deep water, and Jake, acknowledging he cannot catch them swimming, splashes back to shore. But instead of returning to the shack, defeated, he sloshes along the bank in his bare feet.

They're in midstream now, and fairly safe for the moment. Puffing and panting, they regain their breath and let the current carry them. Soon, they believe, he'll tire of following them on foot.

"You pups! You stop!" he yells.

Dicksie makes sure the black valise is in the scow, then nudges Auston, and once again they commence to row.

Jake dodges between trees. "You better stop! You'll tucker out b'fore I do–then I'll catch up an' when I do you're goners, the both of you!"

There is too little moonlight for girl and boy to see him clearly, but they hear him grunting through sand and muck along the water's edge.

"Dicksie–that's no name for a girl. Know why she named you that?" Jake shouts. "B'cause you were s'posed t'be a boy an' she was gonna call you Dick an' then you come along an' she was too dumb an' stubborn ti'give you a proper girl name!"

For a minute or two he curses to himself as fallen

logs bar his way and he must wrestle himself over them.

"An' Auston—that's s'pose t'be t-i-n, not t-o-n! But she couldn't even spell right, your ol' lady was too dumb! You think she was so, so smart an' perfec' —no she wasn't! She was jus' like her litter, like you two—mulehead stubborn! She was ig'orant, ig'orant!"

Taking care to stay in midstream, on they row through the terrible night, pursued by that brutal voice from the shore line, whipped by insult to the memory of their mother. And now, after half a mile of effort, Jake wearies. As he despairs of keeping up with the scow, much less of catching it, he becomes a wild animal, crashing through brush and bellowing his rage.

"Don't b'lieve I'd do it, huh? Well, I will—kill the both of you brats with my bare han's! An' you know why? It ain't jus' that money—oh, I'll get that all right—I'm owed that money by the world—it's 'cause you ain't no real kin t'me an' I got no earthly use for either of you! Now you know, you dirty little devils! You ain't mine an' I wouldn' have you if you was! You're as ig'orant an' stubborn as your ol' lady an' I lay han's on you I'll choke the sneaken', thievin' life outa you an' wrap you in rocks on the bottom of this river!"

Sitting close together, straining at the oars, brother and sister shake and shudder. Never, in the years they have shared a shack with him, have clammed and cleaned and cooked for him, have endured his blows and neglect, have they been as terrified by the man as they are now. For this is a Jake unknown to them. This is a stranger. And the meaning of the stranger's words sinks in. They do not say it to each other, there is no need to.

Their stepfather has gone mad. Insane with greed and alcohol and hate.

If they allow themselves to fall into a madman's clutches, he will really, truly kill.

A splash!

They squint, they see! He's dived into the river! His only hope of catching them is to swim, and swim he does, hauling his bloated body toward them with wild, swift strokes!

They row for their lives!

But they cannot move the cumbersome scow fast enough. Nearer and nearer, churning the brown water into white foam, pulls a hulk of hate, a monster, which seems to be spit up from the bottom by a sickened river. An arm claws at the end of the button boat. Auston ceases to try, surrenders, bursts into sobs. They're lost!

A desperate Dicksie stands. What can she do? How can she defend them? Strike out at the evil thing with an oar?

She tugs at one. It's too heavy!

Suddenly she reaches down, seizes a clam knife, raises it as though to stab! But no! Stumbling over the seat, she lunges along the upright racks, down one side of the scow and up the other, and with long slashes of the knife cuts loose the lines!

Into sixty clamming lines the madman swims! About

his arms they tangle, about his legs, about his body!

He screams! For as he struggles in the net of lines, sixty hooks like needles fasten in his flesh! Hooked, netted, rising halfway out of the water, his mouth opening in agony, he screams as a woman screams:

"Aiiiiiiieeeeeee!"

He sinks!

Into night and a river grave Jake disappears without a trace. The scow drifts on. Brother and sister hear a glug, glug, glug. He's gone.

Overcome with horror at her deed, Dicksie moans, falls, faints dead away.

22. Wherein our heroic heroine and her brave brother part, never to meet again

Dawn.

Mist rises from the river. On its gentle tide the button boat is borne.

In a tree a crow caws, warning the world of winter's coming.

Hidden in cattails, upon her house of weeds and grasses a mother muskrat sits, her children in a circle, teaching them about traps.

Ducks dive and dillydally. As the button boat appears among them in the mist, they flap and scatter.

She wakes. She does not know where she is or what she has done. She does not move, but through the mist she stares about her, her eyes like hands. Beside her lies her brother, sleeping. Under the covered end of the scow is a black valise. Her eyes widen. Lifting her look she sees a row of clamming lines, cut. There is something in her hand, something she has clenched the whole night through. A knife.

She remembers. A cry is torn out of her. Sitting up, she casts the knife away like a hot potato and begins to pound her brother with her fists. "Auston! Auston, wake up!" she implores. "What've I done? What've I done?"

He starts and jumps, beaten out of sleep and forgetting, angry, ready to fight back until he sits and rubs his eyes, until he, too, remembers. Her question hangs between them unanswered. He squints at the shore. "Guess we drifted all night," he says. "We're almost t'town."

"I fainted," she says.

"Fainted?"

"That's what ladies do."

"La-di-da. I thought you was asleep."

She watches ducks dive for their breakfast. He scratches an itch. They cannot look at each other.

"Auston," she whispers.

"What?"

"He's dead."

"Yup. Drownded."

"Drowned. Auston, I have killed our father."

"Some father." He yawns. "He'd of killed us if he could."

She shakes her head. "We aren't sure, we aren't really sure he would, and no one'll ever believe a man would murder his own children. What we do know is he's dead and I did it." She takes a deep, dire breath. "Auston, I'm a murd'ress."

Now his eyes widen. "A murd'ress! What'll you get for that—the 'lectric chair, the hot seat? A murd'ress—wow! They'll fry you like an egg!"

His sister gasps, then plunges her face into her hands and huddles in a heap against the seat of the scow. "Oh, Auston, Auston, I'm so sorry! I didn't mean to hurt him," she moans, "I wouldn't harm a fly! I just meant to keep him from harming us—oh, I'm so wicked and afraid!"

"Me'n my big mouth." Auston's disgusted with himself. "Don't be scared, Dicks," he soothes, "mebbe they'll just lock you up for life."

"Lock me up for life?" Instead of soothing her, the prospect of prison undoes her completely. "Oh, Auston, what'll we do! What'll we ever, ever do!" she groans. She will not weep, but giving way to grief she rocks to and fro, she tears at her long, mousy hair. She is so weakened by hunger, so cramped by days and nights in the cold pit, so sickened by the horror of the night, so tortured by her guilt! All her brother can do is wait, head down, shivering in the early morning breath of autumn.

How alone they are, a boy and girl in a button boat adrift upon a river, how utterly alone and friendless! The hundred-dollar prayers they sent to town in bottles have gone astray. Zip is home, snoring in the shack. Their stepfather is dead, drowned by his own daughter's hand. To what other human being can they turn in their hour of need? To a young peace officer who spanked them in public? To a snobby girl who turned up her nose at them? The terrible truth is that they have no one. They have nothing.

Nothing but the river. The river and its creatures, the river and those toys and treasures they can fish for, the river and its suns and moons. The big brown rope that ties them where they are.

Onward they float, without plan, without hope. A crow caws. A mother muskrat teaches. Ducks dilly-dally. Then the sun rises.

It burns the mist away. It warms the boy, sitting

in the scow, his head bowed. Within the girl, like a match it lights a fire of resolution.

"Auston."

"What?"

"I have made up my mind."

"Oh-oh."

"What a person sets out to do, he ought to finish. So we will." Rising, she sits on one side of the seat and grasps an oar. "Come on, let's both row."

"Row where?"

"To town, Auston."

"Town? You can't go t'town—you're a murd'ress!"

Dicksie sighs. "I know. But you can."

"Me! Go in that burg again?" Summoning up his scorn, he spits ptooey halfway across the river. "You got bats in your belfry! Not on your tintype, I won't!"

Dicksie tosses her head. "You will so. Now sit down and row and I'll tell you why."

He grumps and grumbles but takes his place beside her. Older sisters are born to make up their minds, younger brothers to lose theirs. As the button boat moves steadily downstream in the sunlight, Dicksie explains. It would have been easier, once they hooked the valise, to do as they first dreamed—to keep the money and run away and live happily ever after on movies and popcorn, much easier. But when they discovered it was stolen money belonging to someone else, to return it was the right decision. It showed character. And though she'll admit it's cost them dearly in punishment and danger, even in crime, they must finish what they've started no matter what awful what.

Auston drops his oar. "No matter what awful what?" he demands suspiciously. "What awful what's that mean?"

His sister notices they are now quite close to town. "I merely mean," she says, "that I was the one who really decided to do right, so I should be the one to suffer the consequences, not you."

Auston glowers. "What cons'quences?"

Taking up his oar, she turns the scow and heads it toward the riverbank. When it bumps, she boats the oars. "There." She folds her hands in her lap. "Here's what you must do, Auston. Take the money and walk into town. Take it to the school, not to Whipper Smith or anybody else, and give it to the teachers. Don't mention me at all. Tell them you don't want any reward, just say that instead, you'd rather go to school."

He can't believe his ears. "No reward? Bushwah! School? Abadaba! I thought you was gonna suffer, not me!" Jumping up, he gives the black valise a good kick. "Ow!" He hops about on one bare foot, holding the other. "What awful what is right! An' where'll you be while I'm sufferin'? What'll you do while I'm holdin' the bag?"

She stiffens her upper lip. "Auston, we must part."

"Part?"

"Forever."

"Forever?"

She nods. "I can't go with you. I'm a murd'ress.

Even though I did it to save us, I drowned the only father we had. So I'll go back to the shack and pack and be on my way."

Her seriousness sobers him. "Gosh. My gosh. On your way where?"

She sighs. "I don't know. I'll wander. I'll be a wanderer all my life, an outcast, a fudgetive."

"How'll you earn your keep? There ain't no clams in cities."

"Aren't," she corrects. "Since I can't read nor write much, I'll take in washings, or make rag rugs, or be a flagpole-sitter, or something—I don't know that either. But one thing I do. Auston, we will never see each other again."

"Oh." He is only nine and, until this mournful moment, "never" seemed impossible to him, "forever" only an hour. Now their meaning changes because he does. He grows older. He hangs his head.

"Take good care of Zip, Auston."

"I will."

"And please don't drink or swear or smoke, ever."

"I won't."

"And never forget Her. I never will. Say Her name real often, and so will I, and when we do, wherever we are, She'll be with us and we'll be together."

"Okle-dokle."

She stands. "You must look your best," she says. And wetting the tattered skirt of her curtain dress in the water, using it for a washcloth, she scrubs at his cheeks and chin and pokes into his ears while he

squirms. "There." Bending again, she gives him the black valise.

Button girl and boy stand together in the boat, stand together in the still chill morning. They gaze upon each other for the last time. Their hearts hurt. In the distance, from the town, a schoolbell rings. Auston gulps. Dicksie tries to smile.

"Will you," she whispers, "will you kiss me goodby?"

Auston is too adult now for kissing. Instead, swelling up his GRO-CHICK and squaring his shoulders, he sticks out a manly hand. "Shake, pal," he says.

She takes it, shakes it, holds it. "Farewell, my dear, dear brother."

He pulls it free and, jumping off the shore end of the scow, climbs the bank, turns, and waves. "I'll see bein' ya!" he calls, then trudges off.

Dicksie seizes the oars and rows away as fast as she can, upstream, pinching her eyes shut so that she cannot see him. After a while, however, she can't resist. But it is too late. He is out of sight.

Nor will Auston turn again, even though he wants to madly-badly-sadly. He does, finally, but in vain.

23. Auston marches on

If he had his druthers, before he'd go into this town and hand the valise over to some teachers and ask for an education instead of a hundred big beans, Auston would druther eat ten pounds of chicken necks. Raw. Or be torn to bits by bullets from a submachine gun. Or be tangled in clam lines and sink to the bottom of a river like a sack of cement. Or kiss a girl.

Auston marches on.

He carries the valise as though it contains dynamite rather than six thousand dollars. If the doggone crooks hadn't thrown the doggone money in the drink and if he hadn't had the lousy luck to hook it and if that dumb dodo of a do-right Dicksie hadn't decided they ought to give it back to a bunch of starving widows and orphans–if. But they had and he had and she had and now he's responsible for the whole ding-blasted ball of wax.

Auston marches on.

He passes houses. A sidewalk begins, and his bare feet pad along the unfamiliar surface, rustle through the fallen leaves. When the schoolbell rings again, unexpectedly and now quite near, the clanging almost causes him to collapse. Across the street, lugging heavy loads of books, boys and girls with long faces loiter as though being summoned by the bell to a funeral. Or invited by their parents to a dose of castor oil.

Auston marches on.

Auston stops.

A girl has passed him, a girl with golden curls in a lovely blue dress trimmed with ribbons. Now she stops, turns, and facing him on the sidewalk, bars his way while holding a delicate nose between delicate fingers. "You!" she gasps. He scowls. "I thought I smelled something unspeakable," she chokes. "And I did—you!"

He pretends to be cool as a cucumber. "Hiya, Toots," he says. "Been eatin' many bonbons lately?"

The fair creature stamps a dainty shoe. "And just what, pray tell, are you doing in town again?"

"Goin' t'school."

"School? You? Har-di-har-har," she chuckles. "I told your sister—they'll never accept you because you're dirty and smelly and crude and rude and undoubtedly infested with fleas, flies, lice, mice, bugs, slugs, nits, and zits."

"Oh yeah?" She makes Auston mad enough to tear a telephone book in two. "Oh yeah? Well, they'll take me now!"

"Abadaba."

He advances on her. "They put their peepers on what I got in this v'lise an' they'll be beggin' me on bended knee!"

"Clams, I presume," she sniffs.

"That's right!" he crows. "Six thousan' clams! Six thousan' dollars—the robbery money!"

Diane Estelle Devere is absolutely flabbergasted. The look on her face delights Auston to the tips of his wiggling toes. "That's right, the bank loot everybody

was lookin' for! When the cops was chasin' them robbers they threw it in the river an' me'n Dicksie hooked it up an' we could of kep' it but we got too much char'cter so we sent two big bills in bottles down the river t'let folks know we had it but somebody must of stole 'em or somethin' so I'm takin' it to school so I reckon they will so be glad t'have me Miss Fancypants!"

Diane Estelle Devere has gone white as a ghost, then red as a rose. "Where is your sister, by the bye?" she inquires.

"She couldn't come, she's a mur—" Auston bites his tongue. "She's left home, she's gonna make flagpoles or sit on rag rugs," he bumbles in confusion. "She don't want t'go t'school an' have them boogyladies fill her head with junk till her brain blows up."

The young lady casts a cunning glance at him. "Do you? Do you want to?"

"Sure as Sam Hill don't," he admits. "But I got to. I gotta get rid of this dough."

The princess toys thoughtfully with her golden tresses. Then she smiles at him, disarming him with dimples, luring him with ruby lips. "What was your name? Austin? What a nice name. Let's walk together, Austin," she invites. "Here, I'll help you carry the valise."

Politely she releases her nose, charmingly she helps herself to the handle, and together they set out, the bag between them. Auston is amazed how buttermouth Diane Estelle Devere has become all of a sudden, how palsy-walsy, and what she says as they ankle along amazes him even more. What amazes her, she remarks, is that instead of demanding the hundred-dollar reward in return for the money, he's demanding to be punished for his honesty. In short, to attend school. "Look at them, poor things," she says, pointing at a gaggle of girls here and a brace of boys there. "As soon as they walk through that door, they're not children any more, they're victims."

"Victums?" he asks. "What's that?"

She's only too glad to describe the indescribable tortures that await the youngsters. How they'll soon be prisoners in their seats, their heads crammed with information the way little pigs are stuffed with garbage till they're fat enough to grind into sausages. Some of their skulls, she says, will be so swollen by the day's end that in order to shrink the swelling they must sit bent over half the night, their heads stuck in pails of water, cold water. But the worst thing about school, she confides, is the teachers. "They're fiends," she says.

"Feends?" asks Auston, slowing down. "What's that?"

The fair creature glances about to be sure no one can overhear. "Well, there's Homework Hannah, the English teacher. She gives you so much homework to do every night that you can't get a wink of sleep."

"Yikes," says Auston.

"She's not as horrible as Laura the Lasher though. Laura teaches arithmetic, and if you make even a teentsy mistake in multiplication or long division, she lashes you so black and blue you can't sit down that night to do your English for Homework Hannah or even sit down to stick your head in a pail of cold water."

"Julius H. Priest," says Auston, lagging behind.

"But the fiendiest one of all," whispers his sweet companion, "is Boiler-Room Bessie."

"Boiler-Room Bessie?" Auston breathes. "Oh no."

"Oh yes. She teaches Latin."

"Latun? What's that?"

"It's an old-time language, dead as a doornail now. I'll give you a sample. Ou-yay are-yay an umb-day, irty-day, elly-smay at-bray."

"Come again?"

"You are an intelligent, mannerly, handsome boy."

Auston isn't really listening. He's caught a case of the galloping fidgets. "What about Boiler-Room Bessie?"

She edges closer, lowering her voice. "Well, in the winter, when the boilers in the basement are heating the school, if you don't do your Latin perfectly, Bessie takes you down to the boilers, which are hotter than Hades in the summertime, and ties you with straps and pulls you closer and closer until—"

"No!" Auston howls as though on fire, letting go of the valise. "Don't tell me no more!" He sits smack-dab down on the sidewalk, sweat pouring out of him like grease. "I ain't goin'!" he squawks, mopping at his forehead. "I cain't go!" He looks wildly about him at the children, the innocent victims. "What'll I do!" he groans.

Fluttering her lashes, Diane Estelle Devere arranges

an expression of pity on her pretty face. "I don't know, poor boy," she sympathizes. "Even if you just return the money and keep mum about school, they'll grab you and enroll you anyway—You're lost."

Auston's eyes roll in his head. "Holy Toledo!"

Letting him stew in his own juice for a moment, his lovely helpmate works up another expression, this one of sacrifice. When she speaks, it's softly as a caterpillar coughing into a cotton handkerchief. She's changed her mind about him, she declares, she wants to be his true friend, and honesty and character such as his should be rewarded. Therefore she's thought of a simply epizootic idea.

"Epizootic?"

"Wonderful. If you want me to, Austin," she offers, "I'll take the valise to school for you."

He's on his feet like a rocket! "You will?"

"Then you'll be free as the breeze."

"I will?"

"I'll even collect the reward for you and make sure you get it."

"You will?" He hesitates. "Golly, I dunno. Dicks told me to do it myself."

"Did I mention Dave the Dipper?"

"Who?"

"The janitor. He dips the children."

"Dips 'em?"

"He has a tank in the basement, like a big bathtub, and when someone smells of something unpleasant, like clams—"

"Clams?"

"Dave drags them down to the tank, which is full of the same gooey, poisony stuff they dip sheep in, makes them strip naked, then pushes them headfirst into—"

"Here!" Auston's heard enough. He shoves the valise into her arms. "So long! Toodle-oo! Ta-ta! Thanks a lot, Diane! Don't take no wooden nickels!" And down the street and around a corner lickety-split he flies, far, far from school.

The second he disappears, Diane Estelle Devere opens the black bag. She smiles as do the angels. Then, on a thought, she reaches down, slips a hundred-dollar bill from her shoe, the very bill she found floating in a bottle on the river, drops it into the valise, snaps and straps the bag shut, and starts again for school. She'd intended, this very afternoon in fact, to begin spending the hundred dollars on cherry phosphates, but why shouldn't she add it now to the rest of the loot? After all, in a few minutes she'll have it back anyway, and as a reward from a grateful town.

She skips.

Auston runs till he is out of breath and out of town. He may not have turned the money over in person, as Dicksie warned him to do, but at least he's passed it on to a true friend, and by now it's safely at the school, he tells himself, and that's the important thing. But what if Diane Estelle Devere isn't truly a true friend?

He scuffs along the highway, his raggedy trousers flapping, headed for home sweet home. He'll take care of Zip, he'll never drink or smoke or swear, but neither will he ever set foot in that terrible town again. Surely no one, not even an older sister, can blame a boy if his favorite fun is something else besides being yanked or spanked or shot or whatnot or whipped or dipped or made to sit with his head in a pail of cold water. But what if Diane Estelle Devere doesn't give him the hundred-dollar reward?

He hardens himself. Around himself he forms a shell strong enough to keep out every doubt and fear. But then, as he trudges along, something slips inside the shell, something sharp stabs him in his core. It is the knife of conscience. What if Diane Estelle Devere keeps all the stolen money for herself, all of it? What if he's done his dear sister wrong? What if he's let the memory of his mother down?

Screaming "Eeeeeeee!" inside his shell, Auston marches on.

24. Father, dear Father, come home with me now!

Slowly, solemnly the button boat goes. Up the river Dicksie rows.

She wonders if Auston has done his duty and returned the money to the school in person and is at this moment sitting in his first class learning to read or write or count and glad to be there.

She wonders if she has enough strength left to reach the shack, and if, when she does, there will be some food for her.

She wonders what to pack, to take with her on her wanderings. She owns so pitifully little! The dress she has on, a pair of rubber boots with holes, half of a comb. And oh, she almost forgot. That will be a comfort to her wherever she may be, a source of love and hope and remembering—the framed motto: GOD BLESS OUR HAPPY HOME. But no, she mustn't take it, she must leave it for Auston, who will need it even more.

She passes the path that leads through the woods to the Pretend School. Why not take some of the dried-out movie magazines stored there, so that she can read them in the lonely evenings and recall the happy hours spent teaching Auston and the bottle boys and girls? But no, she can't read, and now, giving up an education, she never will! Auston will, however. She must leave them, too, for him.

She wonders what she can ever do to keep body and soul together. Scrub floors? Lick postage stamps? Sell vacuum cleaners door to door? Demonstrate potato peelers on a corner? What is a clammer's daughter prepared to do? Beg?

Dicksie cries out. Here—this is where it happened! This is where he swam after them, where she cut the lines, where he sank!

She drops the oars, drops to her knees, and leans out over the water, staring into the brown and awful depths. She seems to hear that final glug, glug, glug, she seems to see that flabby body rolling with the current, over and over on the weedy bottom—torn eternally by barbs of steel, tied eternally in its grave, fed upon forever by the fishes! Father, dear Father, she cries within herself, come home with me now! Rise from the river alive and well and say I'm not a murd'ress! Forgive your little girl!

Answer is there none. Onward the river rolls, keeping to itself its secrets, its cans and clams and crimes.

In the silence she stands and wrings her hands. If she were an Indian princess, she might end it all by taking a lover's leap over a cliff. If she were a woman, she might become a gangster's gun moll and die in a hail of hot lead. If she were a man, she might enlist in the Foreign Legion and disappear into the desert. She sighs. She takes her seat once more and lays limp hands upon the oars. And as she touches them, to row upon her weary, wretched, wanderer's way, all the sighables of her small life combine to overwhelm her, turning on her tender waterworks.

At last, at last, while she is alone and unobserved, our Dicksie weeps. Buckets. She weeps—but keeps on rowing.

25. A clam by any other name, even by the name of Diane Estelle Devere, would smell as clammy

"I found it! I found it!"

Into the schoolyard skips Diane Estelle Devere, her eyes sparkling, her golden curls flying. Over her head she raises the black valise like a banner. "I found it! I found it!"

"What? Found what?" Boys and girls come running, to cluster about her.

"The money! The robbery money!" she proclaims.

Oohs and ahs! The news spreads like measles. "Hey, Diane's found it! Lucky Diane!"

Children rush from the school. Teachers rush from the school, smiling and pleased. None of them looks as though she'd give her classes too much homework or lash them black and blue or strap them to a burning boiler. The janitor rushes up from the basement. His hands are clean, not stained with kid-dip. The principal rushes from his office. In seconds the schoolyard is crowded and swirling with an excited throng. The bell clangs a final clang, but no one hears it. In minutes the mayor arrives, and the town council, for in a small village like this, news travels like greased lightning, by shout and telephone, through windows and over back fences. Dogs bark it, birds twitter, and cats meow. And last but not least, rushing up on his motorcycle to make the occasion official, here comes Peace Officer Whipper Smith!

The center of attention, the girl of the hour, is Diane Estelle Devere. Everyone's been searching for the loot, everyone wants to know how in the dickens she found it and where. And the fair creature tells them, being modest and proud at the same time, which is a very difficult thing to be. "I never gave up, I kept thinking of the starving widows and orphans in the city who needed this money desperately," she says, while everyone hushes. "After all, there is a Depression going on, though I must say my parents and I don't care a Fig Newton. So I just went on searching and searching, every day after school and Saturday and Sunday. I hunted through the woods along the highway till my delicate skin was scratched and bleeding, till I was worn to a frazzle, till I fainted." Everyone clucks with admiration. "But each time I picked myself up and went on with the search, for I have simply oodles of sticktoitiveness and other good qualities too numerous to mention. So last evening, just as it was getting dark and I was stumbling through a briar patch and feeling faint again, I found it. And here it is," she says, holding up the black bag. "In conclusion, I want you to know I found it not for myself, but for all the dear, humble citizens of this dear, humble town." She curtsies. "I thank you one and all, and I shall be glad to sign autographs at any time."

Cheers go up, three cheers for Diane Estelle Devere.

A path is cleared for Whipper Smith. Handsome as ever in his gray whipcord uniform and leather boots, he strides forward to take official possession of the loot in order to transfer it to the city bank from which it was stolen.

She hands it over.

He accepts it.

Dimpling, her eyes downcast, shyly she touches his sleeve. "Officer Smith," she reminds him, "isn't there a hundred-dollar reward for whoever found the money? It isn't for me, really," she adds, thinking of thousands of cherry phosphates trickling down her delicate gullet. "I intend to give every penny of it to the poor."

"Bet your boots there is," he says. "And you shall have it this minute if not quicker."

While everyone holds his breath, he unbuckles and opens the black valise. He peers inside, smiling. With one gauntlet glove he reaches in, fishes about, and removes a hundred-dollar bill. He raises it high. Practically no one present has seen a hundred-dollar bill in years, if ever.

Diane Estelle Devere extends a dainty hand.

But wait! What's this?

Whipper Smith stops. Everyone stares.

His nose wrinkles. His ears twitch. His blue eyes water.

"Phweee-ewww!" he snorts. "That's the awfullest, rottenest, powerfulest smell I ever smelt!"

He stares at the bill. "Wait just a darn minute here." He lowers his nose into the valise and sniffs a

long, strong sniff. "I smell a rat—I mean a clam—I mean those kids!" he cries. "Those two kids in the middle of Main Street the day the crooks came through—remember, folks?" he asks the crowd. Everyone nods. "Remember how I had to save 'em and they saved me?" He shoots a suspicious look at the lovely child before him. "This is how they smelt—you'd never smell like this, would you?"

"Of course not!" snaps Diane Estelle Devere. "I take a bath every day—a bubble bath!"

It's a slip of the lip. She turns white as snow, then red as a fire engine.

"Aha!" cries Whipper Smith detectively. "Then where'd you get this money? From those kids, didn't you? They found it, didn't they?"

Curses, thinks our villainess—foiled! She's furious. She's out-foxed herself. She's lost the reward and, even worse, she's been stupid enough to lose the hundred dollars she put back in the bag on the way to school! And now she's disgraced, caught in a crackerjack of a lie in front of the entire town! She has only her persnickety pride left, but she has plenty of that.

"I don't care pooh," says she, cold as ice and twice as natural. "After all, they're only clammers."

"Shame on you, Miss McNasty!" says Whipper Smith.

Teachers and mayor and town council tsk-tsk at her. The other children hiss and stick out their tongues.

Suddenly something strikes Peace Officer Smith. Since the day the gangsters came and he made a blithering idiot of himself, he's had only two chances to strut his stuff before the town. One afternoon he stopped a dogfight and one morning he caught a hobo heisting an old maid's corset off her washline and took him to jail and felt sorry for him and gave him a free bed for the night and let him go. The rest of his time he's spent waiting for more gangsters to arrive and figuring out what he'd do if they did, which they haven't. But now, at last, he has a task, a real honest-to-gosh police duty!

"Saved by a nose!" he shouts. "What the razzle-dazzle am I doing here? I gotta find those kids—they're the real heroes!" He buckles up the black valise—jams his hat on his head—rushes through the crowd, the bag under his arm—hops on his mighty Harley-Davidson—starts it—stops it—rushes back stammering, "But I dunno where to find 'em—must be a dozen clammers living on the river—anybody here got an idee where?"—grows more flustered than ever when Diane Estelle Devere swirls her curls and sneers, "Who cares where? They're still stinkpots. Just follow your nose."—rushes again to the motorcycle—hops on—kicks the starter again—grabs one handle bar and, still clutching the bag under his arms, guns the motor—starts off in an explosion of laughter and a cloud of dust—stops—blushes as plain as an elephant's proboscis because he's forgotten to raise his kickstand—kicks it up—hunches down and throttles away a' though tin cans are tied to his tail!

26. Nooooooo!

She reaches the cove. She beaches the button boat. Now she must bid farewell to the only home she has ever known.

She pauses for a moment to have a last, loving look at the wreck surrounded by a mess, at the shack and the beer bottle pile and the clamshell pile and the insides pile and the billion buzzing flies.

She sighs. Moisture fills her eyes. She dries them on her sleeve, then picks her woeful way between the piles to the shack.

She opens the door.

She shrieks.

"Nooooooo!"

For out of a mound of filthy muskrat skins, up, up, up it looms! A thing! A monstrous thing of tangled hair and yellow fangs and red, red eyes! A thing of overalls and ocean and airplane and Lucky Lindy and dried blood and fishhooks hanging from its face and neck and shoulders!

Across the shack it crashes, smashing through and over table, chair, and boxes! Its maw opens wide, it roars like a beast! Now it lunges for her, reaches for her with its hairy, bloody, fishhook arms as if to seize, to crush, to eat its own young!

The panic-stricken child would retreat if she could,

would flee if her legs would support her, but the world grows dim to her, darkens, spins!

Will she swoon? And swooning, fall into the clutches of the thing?

27. The most tee-legged, toe-legged, triple-dip, bow-legged thrill in the world!

Along the highway, raggedy trousers flapping, bare feet hurting, Auston marches on.

He hears a hornet's whir, behind him, which in another instant becomes a growl of cylinders, a blast of exhaust. He swivels.

That motorcycle! That man in uniform, after him again!

What'll he do? Climb a tree? Dig a hole and crawl in and pull the hole in after him?

Auston does the only thing he can—dives headfirst into a whortleberry bush. But too late. He's been spotted. The Harley-Davidson screeches brakes, swerves, stops, and Peace Officer Whipper Smith leaps off, thrusts a glove into the bush, and snatches poor Auston out by the seat of his pants. "Lemme alone!" he bawls.

Standing him upright, Whipper Smith grins from ear to ear. "Just the rapscallion I'm looking for!"

"Go take a flyin' jump at a rollin' doughnut!" Auston bawls.

"I don't mean rapscallion, I mean hero!" grins the young officer. "Got the bank money right here"—he pats the valise under his arm—"and the whole town knows you and your sis found it—you're both heroes! Say, where is she?"

This is too much for Auston. Had he been licked, he could have endured it. Had he been shot at or lied to or laughed at or run down or cast out by a crowd of nose-holders, he'd have been prepared for that too. But not this sudden switch. To see the money where it's supposed to be, and on top of that to be praised, is too much. He blinks, his lower lip quivers and, breaking down, he begins to cry with all his lungpower as might any tired, hungry, lonely, frightened nine-year-old.

"Dicksie run away!" he sobs. "I hooked the money outa the river an' she said we oughta give it back an' we tried but Jake wanted t'keep it an' come after us an' she killed 'im an' I brung it t'town an' that girl hornswoggled it outa me an' Dicksie's run away t'make rag rugs an' sit on flagpoles!" He flings his arms about the Peace Officer's legs and hugs him. "So I'll never see 'er again 'cause she's a murd'ress!"

"Rag rugs? Hornswoggled? She's Jake's girl? Murderess? Flagpoles? Jake's dead? Run away?" So befuddled by this mishmash is Whipper that he puts a glove on the boy's head and scratches Auston's head instead of his own! "A murderess? Not that girl, nosirree," he says. But one part of the story comes clear to him. "Run away? She can't run away! We've got to catch her, stop her, and fast—c'mon, shake a leg!"

He hoists Auston, and with the black bag under one arm and the sobbing boy under the other, wrig-

gling like a greased pig, sprints to the motorcycle, plunks him down on the fender over the rear wheel, shouts at him to hang on, hang on, they're off to the races, sets the siren wailing, guns the great black and silver machine, and away they go!

Out of the depths of despair, Auston is rocketed to a heaven of happiness. His eyes are full of rushing air, his ears are full of motor thunder and siren scream, his behind is full of heat and bounce, and his arms are full of a big, strong, fatherly friend who's going to help! Hanging on for dear life, he hopes the ride never ends! It's the most tee-legged, toe-legged, triple-dip, bow-legged thrill in the world! It's epizootic!

When they near the turnoff onto the snake-track road through the woods, he kicks Whipper's boot and they screech to a stop and leap off and Auston stutters down that road, that's where we live, down that road by the river, and the Peace Officer lights out on a dead run with the black valise under his arm and the boy at his heels.

Will they reach the shack in time? Can they save our Dicksie from a fearsome fate?

28. Who's chasing who?

They reach the cove.

What the? What kind of an utty-nay, azy-cray, ame-gay is this? Round the mulberry bush?

But no, in a second they see, it's a deadly race between daughter and stepfather! Round and round the beer bottle pile and the clamshell pile and the insides pile, Dicksie scampers for her life! While after her in his overalls, arms outstretched to seize her, hooks and lines still hanging from his bloody face and neck and shoulders, runs a huge and maddened Jake!

Peace Officer Smith and Auston stand in shock for another second, frozen, helpless. Then the officer drops the valise.

"Halt!" he hollers. "Stop! Whoa!" And when the race continues, he enters it himself, chasing after Jake, who's chasing Dicksie!

Auston's left alone and doesn't want to be! Anxious to keep close to the protection of his new friend, he follows him, chasing after Whipper Smith, who's chasing Jake, who's chasing Dicksie!

And now, waked out of a sound sleep by the commotion, out of the shack runs Zip, barking and howling, and chases after Auston, who's chasing Whipper Smith, who's chasing Jake, who's chasing Dicksie!

Round and round they go, round and round the

beer bottle pile and the clamshell pile and the insides pile, faster and faster, hollering and crying and roaring and barking—a living merry-go-round! A desperate game of follow-the-leader—but who's the leader? For now the circle is joined, and Dicksie—who's being chased by Jake, who's being chased by Whipper, who's being chased by Auston, who's being chased by Zip —Dicksie's chasing Zip!

She catches him, passes him, trips over Zip! Jake lunges for her!

When with a battle shout, and with the same gumption and energy which once lifted a cow into a steeple, Whipper Smith catches the button boatman —throws both young, strong arms around him in a grip of iron—lifts him—hurls him!

Into the beer bottle pile? No?

Into the clamshell pile? No?

Where, then?

No, no, a thousand times no—not into that!

29. In which greed and cruelty and good-for-nothingness get their comeuppance, while truth and honesty and gumption are rewarded

Yes, into that! Into the great, gray glob of glue he goes! Into the icky, sticky mountain of the slippery, slimy, moldy, maggoty insides of a million clams or more! Jake thrashes and splashes and stinks and sinks!

Gasping at her narrow escape, Dicksie stumbles to her rescuer and grabs him by one leg while Auston grabs him by the other and together the three stand staring at the insides pile.

A hand appears. Then a foot. And then, squishing slowly up like a fat and poisonous toadstool, a head and a whiskery face. As it rises, the billion flies that hover over the insides pile by day and night, buzzing with wonder and delight, settle down upon it to play hide-and-seek in ears and eyes and nose and whiskers.

The mouth opens. In scoots a fly. "Bleah!" snorts Jake in disgust, spitting it out.

"Oh, Father," Dicksie says to him, "I thought I'd drowned you!"

"I thought you run away!" says Auston to her.

"I thought you told me you didn't have chick nor child!" says Whipper to Jake.

"I thought mebbe that snobby Diane swiped the money!" Auston says to Whipper.

"I thought I asked you to take it straight to school!" says Dicksie to her brother.

"I thought–" says Whipper.

"I thought–" says Auston.

"I thought–" says Dicksie.

"I thought kids is s'pose t'mind their folks!" Jake roars. "An' peace officers is s'pose t'keep the peace!"

Whipper Smith stiffens his back and straightens his hat. "That's just what I aim to do, Jake," says he. "And I'll start by telling you that you are a shiftless, ornery, good-for-nothing old rip. You have two dandy kids here, honest as the day is long. They saved my life the day those gangsters came through town and they returned the bank money to its rightful owners and you better start appreciating them and loving them and being a good father to them or I'll haul you out of there and clap you in the town clink for child neglect and just plain natural-born cussedness!"

Jake blinks. He knows he's beaten. He sniffles and snuffles and wheezes and brushes away two tears and ten flies and goes into the performance that Dicksie and Auston know so well.

"Whipper, you are right, lad, you are speakin' the truth an' just a-tearin' my poor ol' heart out!" he blubbers. "I been as rotten as these here clam guts, but as sure's the Lord above's my witness, an' also their dear dead Momma, I'll reform an' turn over a new leaf an' I'll be the sweetes', lovines' daddy t'these little darlin's you ever did see! You just wait'n watch if I ain't!"

Whipper shakes his head. "Sorry, Jake, I can't wait. You're going to start this minute if not sooner."

"Oh, I will, I will," Jake promises. "You jus' say 'er an' I'll do 'er."

"Okay, from now on you'll earn your living and theirs by yourself. You'll do all the clamming."

"All?" says Jake. "You mean work?"

"I mean work. Another thing, don't give that dog another drop of beer."

"Zip? No beer?" cries Jake. "He'll dry up'n die of thirst!"

"I won't have a drunkard dog in my town."

The button boatman's in deeper than he realized. "But if he don't drink for show, how'll I get free beers?"

"You won't," smiles Whipper, "and you won't have time anyways. You'll be too busy clamming."

"Oh," says Jake. "I forgot."

"But the biggest thing," says the peace officer, "is school."

"School?" says Jake.

"School!" cries Dicksie.

"School?" groans Auston.

"As of tomorrow morning," says Whipper Smith, "these youngsters are coming in town to school, every dagnab day. Which reminds me," he adds, freeing himself from the children and stepping smartly around the piles. Taking up the black valise, he parades back to Dicksie, opens the bag, takes out a bill and raises it high above her. "And now, ma'am, on behalf of the town and the police and the bank and the city and the President and the whole U.S. of A., I present you with the reward. One hundred smackeroos. And you deserve every smacker."

At the sight of the good, crisp, new green, Jake sits up and takes notice, exposing his tattooed chest. A fly flits aboard the airplane and buzzes through the clouds of hair, over the ocean with Lucky Lindy.

Auston swallows hard.

Bowing low, Peace Officer Smith presents the bill.

"Thank you kindly, sir," says Dicksie. "Mercy," she says, "what'll I ever, ever do with so much?"

"Steak?" suggests Jake.

"Bubble gum?" suggests Auston.

"Well," suggests Whipper, "was I you, I'd buy me and my brother some nifty clothes for school. And some good strong soap for when you take a bath before school tomorrow." He grins down at her. "And what do you say to that, young lady?"

Dicksie gazes up at her champion, her gallant knight of nowadays. In the small clam of her world, she has indeed found a real pearl. His badge is so bright, his baby-blue eyes so twinkly, his towhead so tow, his grin so absolutely yummy! She pictures him on the silver screen in a movie theayter, riding after rustlers faster than Tom Mix, and suffocating Greta Garbo with kisses! Gazing at him, she gets dizzy again.

"Oooooooo," she breathes, blushing.

"What say?" he asks her.

"I love you," she says.

30. It will so

Down-river floats the button boat. In and out of sun it drifts, in and out of shade. It is a face seen in a dark mirror, a whisper heard in a dream.

"What a beautiful day," says Dicksie.

"Bushwah," says Auston.

"It is so," she insists.

A line tautens. While she backwaters the oars, Auston hops over her seat, hauls up the line, pries off the clam, then lowers the line and returns to his end of the scow. They haven't spoken much this early morning, but they have done a great deal of thinking.

"What a mean man," Auston says. "He'll never die—he'll just mean away. I knew he'd take the reward soon's Whipper was gone."

"So did I." Dicksie sighs. "But we must try to think of him as kindly as we can. He's the only Poppa we have."

"Abadaba," says Auston.

Nothing, it seems, has changed for them. As soon as the coast was clear yesterday, Jake floundered out of the insides pile, took the hundred dollars away from Dicksie and knocked them both a few good ones for old times' sake. He'd have to let 'em start school, he declared, because that whippersnapper of a Whipper Smith'd be lookin' for 'em in town, nothin' he could do 'bout that, but they was t'clam t'school an' clam home an' clam every day they wasn't in school an' the rest of the time he'd work 'em down t'nubbins. Jake was spending today in bed with Zip, resting and drinking beer.

And yet, everything has changed, for brother and sister are actually on their way to town, on the way to the first day of school in their lives.

They steal secret glances at each other, seeing themselves for the first time through the eyes of other children—Dicksie in her unhemmed lace-curtain dress and rubber boots, Auston in his raggedy pants and holey boots and GRO-CHICK shirt. They are very quiet.

"Dicks?"

"What?"

"Do we really stink somethin' awful?"

"I guess we do, Auston. We've been around clams so long we're used to it, but other folks aren't. So I guess we do smell to them."

He thinks about that. "But listen," he argues, "if we gave all that money back to the widows an' orphans, if we showed char'cter an' done right, won't that make us smell better?"

"Did right," she corrects. Younger brothers have the bad habit of asking questions that older sisters cannot possibly answer. But she cannot tell a lie. "No," she says finally, "but we'll be better. And being better's better than smelling better."

"Nertz," he says.

"It is so," she insists.

"Not to a nose, it ain't," says he.

They are silent again, thinking. They pass a moss meadow where a herd of cows wade in shallow water drinking and washing and brushing their teeth before breakfast. The young heifers lick and flick and make themselves as attractive as they can, while the teen-age bulls butt their heads together and pretend not to notice.

"Auston!" Dicksie rests the oars. "Auston, I just had a weenie!"

"Weenie?"

"An idea! You'll see!" And swiftly she sends the scow downstream, to a woods, to a familiar path which leads through the woods. "C'mon!" she says, beaching the boat.

Hitching up her skirt, running, she leads him to the surprise glade lovely with sunlight, noisy with birds, and busy with bugs. They stop, staring about them for a minute at the Pretend School, at the cardboard desk and the rows of bottle children.

"Now," says Dicksie in her old teachery way, "here's what we'll do. There must be a little leftover beer in every bottle. You do half and I'll do half—pour what's in each bottle into one bottle."

Auston scowls. "What the heck for?"

"You'll see," she says brightly, and sets to work at once.

There are a few drops in each bottle, and when brother and sister have poured them out, collecting them in two bottles, then combining them in one, Dicksie holds a bottle almost half full of flat, stale, buggy beer. "See what I have," she smiles. "Perfume!"

"Perfume?"

"Don't you remember? Whipper said to buy some soap and take baths before we start school. Well," she explains, "Poppa took the money for clothes and soap and he wouldn't let us take a bath anyways, but perfume's stronger than soap—we'll use this and cover up the clam smell!"

Auston's doubtful. "You sure?"

"Sure I'm sure," she assures him. And cupping his hands, she pours out the dregs and shows him how to splash them freely over his face and neck and even behind his dirty ears, doing the same for herself in a more ladylike manner. "There," she smiles, primping her mousy hair and posing as though she were a hoity-toi Diane Estelle Devere in a pretty dress sipping pink lemonade made in the shade. "Aren't we classy, Auston?"

He sniffs at himself, tries to nod, then explodes. "Wow! Phew!" he chokes. "That's awful—now we don't even smell like people, we smell like Zip!"

"We do not," Dicksie says.

"We stink like ol' flea-bit drunken dogs!"

Dicksie's gray eyes brim with tears, but she will not weep. "You hush," she says.

Auston looks at his sister, then shakes his head with a new respect. "Beer perfume," he says. "I can't figger you out, Dicks. Mebbe I never will. But either you're really dumb or—" He makes her wait.

"Or what?"

"Or you're really somethin' special."

She smiles again, takes his hand and gives it a tiny

squeeze of thanks, and together they leave the Pretend School forever, drifting down-river again in silence, thinking.

They hear the town. There are houses and a water tower and a smokestack and a church steeple. They hear the horns of automobiles, and a schoolbell calling. Dicksie steers the scow to shore and Auston fastens it to a tree trunk. Climbing the bank, they turn for a final, lingering look at the button boat, at its limp lines and scummy bottom, at its leaky, water-beaten sides and square, ugly ends. They look and look. They can scarcely tear themselves away. To their surprise, now that they may actually leave it, may actually escape for a few hours, they're not certain whether to be glad or sad, whether to jump for joy or be down in the dumps.

Suppose you are a small girl and boy, minding your own business in the mud. Something tickles you, a dream perhaps, or perhaps a sharp steel hook. Life can be very hard and lonely on the bottom. So you open your shell and suck the dream or the hook or whatever-it-is inside to taste and—yank! Before you can say "Wait!" or "What the holy tomato goes on here?" you are out of your button boat and being pried open whether you want to be or not and dropped into a crowd of strangers whether you want to be or not and that is almost the end of you but not quite.

Auston's imagination is running away with him like a motorcycle. Thinking about Homework Hannah and Laura the Lasher and Boiler-Room Bessie and Dave the Kid-Dipper, he breaks out into goose bumps.

What'll they say when they discover he can't read or write a lick? What'll they do when they get a snootful of this beer perfume? Will they forgive him if he can wiggle ten toes one at a time? Is spitting accurately and loudly through gaps in your teeth considered by teachers as important as arithmetic?

My dream's come true at last, Dicksie tells herself, and Lily's too, at least partly true. Over and over she assures herself that school will be simply wonderful. The other children will so like us, she promises herself, no matter what we wear or how we smell. But the marvelous thing is that now, Depression and all, we'll be like other boys and girls everywhere, learning and making friends and growing up to be clean, decent men and women. Now, instead of being nameless, useless clams ourselves, we'll be turned into bright, shiny buttons. And when we are, she vows, if hard times ever happen again, if things should ever come undone again or fall apart, we'll help to fasten them together, Auston and me. We'll learn and work and help to button up the world.

"Oh, Auston," she sighs happily, "won't it be just scrumptious!"

"Banana oil," says Auston.

"It will so," says the gritty girl. "It will so."